HOW SMART ARE YOU?

TEST YOUR OWN IQ

HOW SMART ARE YOU?

TEST YOUR OWN IQ

NORMAN SULLIVAN

BLACK DOG & LEVENTHAL PUBLISHERS
NEW YORK

Designed by Martin Lubin.

This 1994 edition is published by arrangement with Sterling Publishing Company, Inc. by

Black Dog & Leventhal Publishers Inc.
151 West 19th Street
New York, New York 10011

Distributed by

Workman Publishing Company
708 Broadway
New York, New York 10003

Manufactured in the United States of America

ISBN: 0-9637056-1-X

Third Printing, August, 1994

CONTENTS

INTRODUCTION

How smart are you? Have you ever taken an IQ test? What is intelligence, anyway? What has it to do with intuition, imagination, creativity—or any of the other special talents we honor? How can we quantify such a concept?

Any measure of intelligence inevitably involves a complex set of assumptions about what intelligence is and how it is valued in our society. Surveys have shown that most people rate intelligence amongst the highest values, along with health and wealth. Although tests of Intelligence Quotient, or IQ, have outgrown their original purpose (to predict academic success), they have survived and maintain a high status because they measure a quality deemed of great importance in society.

For more than a century, IQ tests have evoked controversy and met with conflict at every turn. The significance of the test and the fact that it provides a "scale" for intelligence has aroused highly charged emotions. Theories have been propounded that intelligence is influenced by environment, especially in the formative years, and by other factors. But heredity and environment never work in isolation; they always work in interaction with each other. So the primary argument comes down to determining what the ratio of the IQ score is.

IQ tests have been implemented in American education, and have been used in schools, colleges, graduate programs, businesses, and corporations. At the outset it may seem useful and fortunate that we have a standardized measure with which to gauge people. Unfortunately, however, no one has been able to fully substantiate the correlation between IQ tests and intelligence.

Even if we separate IQ tests from the issue of intelligence, can we condone using the scores as a basis to select an individual for a particular position? This façade of practical usefulness of IQ tests may shroud a much deeper, fundamental problem in our society. Users of IQ tests must ask exactly what it is measuring, and whether the tests measures the same thing for all subjects. The most frequent and vehement attack against IQ tests is the charge that they are culturally biased against racial and ethnic minorities and the poor. No one test can be completely "objective" no matter how hard the test maker tries.

We have attempted to make our book as "culturally neutral" as possible. This just means minimizing "culture loading" by avoiding the use of words or pictures that are more accessible to one group than another. Neutral elements used may include lines, curves, squares and circles—involving universal concepts such as up/down, open/closed, right/left, whole/half, full/empty, larger/smaller, many/few, etc. More complex problems involve relational reasoning of figure-series completions and figural analogies.

Questions involving reasoning and deduction questions require you to examine a given premise and infer conclusions from that premise. Verbal skills tested involve knowing the meaning of words and how to spell them. Of course, the section requires some education and experience, so it is much more culturally loaded than some other areas. We have included these sections to make the tests more fun and challenging, while still eliminating highly biased entries.

FORMAT

In this book there are three sections—Elementary, Challenging and Masterful, with sixty questions in each of the first two sections and forty-five in the third. The tests are meant to amuse and challenge you, certainly taxing your cerebral capacity.

The example below shows one type of question you'll find. It is not a conclusive representation of question types, but it does give you a clue into how the test requires you to think, and what kinds of things you should look for.

A popular type of question is to choose the 'odd one out' from a group of words, shapes, symbols, etc. The testmaker must take care to ensure that the 'odd one out' has an outstanding difference from the others and that the distractors (the choices that are not 'odd') are similar enough to the correct one to provide some challenge. Here is an example of the type of question which should not be given, because it would give rise to disagreement:

Which is the odd one out?

3 4 5 6 7 8

At first glance, there is no apparent answer. It is no use choosing any one number on the grounds that it is odd, even, or a prime number, since there are three of each. They all follow a straightforward arithmetic progression, so there is no clue there. What then is left? Let's spell out the numbers:

three four five six seven eight

Any clue here? Four—because the number of letters corresponds with the number itself; five—because it contains V, the Roman numeral for the number itself; eight—because it is the only word that starts with a vowel. You could think of other possible answers, but they are all weak, simply because no one number has any distinctive feature.

Here is a better example:

Which is the odd one out?

6 7 10 15 20 21

Your reasoning could follow these lines: is there a common divisor in all but one number? No. Is there a single odd or even number? No. What about a common sequence? No—as they increase by 1, 3, 5, 5, 1. Nothing outstanding there. What then, is the only number in the series that has a characteristic not shared by the others? The only such number is 7, because it is the only prime number. This is the sort of reasoning you will have to practice as you go through the tests. We are not trying to trick you; we are trying to challenge you.

You should begin by gathering writing materials—not only because some of the problems may require working-out on paper, but also because you should keep note of your answers and scores (these appear at the end of each individual test) until you have completed all the tests. At the end of the book is a scoring chart with instructions on how to figure out your actual IQ, gauging your scores in relation to the majority of people in your age group.

Have a watch or clock handy so that you can carefully time yourself when you begin each test. Speed of answering is related to speed of comprehension, so each test has a time limit. A correct answer arrived at with little delay shows quicker comprehension, yet it is better to linger a while and arrive at the correct answer than to give the wrong answer quickly.

When the time limit is up you shouldn't record any more answers, even if you have not completed the test. For your own interest you may continue to the end of that particular test. The charm of this book is that you can choose to take tests adhering to the time limits, or you may prefer to go through the tests without regard to the time, simply viewing them as entertainment and pleasure—just as you would tackle a crossword puzzle to pass the time, in no particular hurry.

We hope to have offered brain-teasers you will find exciting and enlightening, while also providing you with an IQ scale you can use to measure and compare with others'. Remembering that the IQ number game gauges what we have already learned, and not our capacity to learn, we can take advantage of it for more enjoyable and entertaining purposes.

GROUP I

ELEMENTARY

TEST I

Time limit: 25 minutes

1 Pair words in the first column with words in the second column, finishing with nine pairs.

(1) TENNIS	(A) WORK
(2) SAFETY	(B) STORE
(3) HOUSE	(C) CLAD
(4) SHOP	(D) BENCH
(5) SEE	(E) MATCH
(6) BAND	(F) LOCK
(7) IRON	(G) SAW
(8) WORK	(H) AGE
(9) TOY	(I) HOLD

2 Which of these wrought-iron gates differs from the others?

3 What two terms complete this series?

A I D 4 H 8 M 13 – –

4 What names are these?

(A) O P S N B O
(B) K T K U
(C) D Q Q H
(D) V M G L E V H

5 Which is the odd one out?

(A) GRAND	(F) BEN FRANKLIN
(B) TEN-SPOT	(G) CLAM
(C) BUCK	(H) GREENBACK
(D) RAND	(I) FIVER
(E) C-NOTE	

6 Which scroll is wrong?

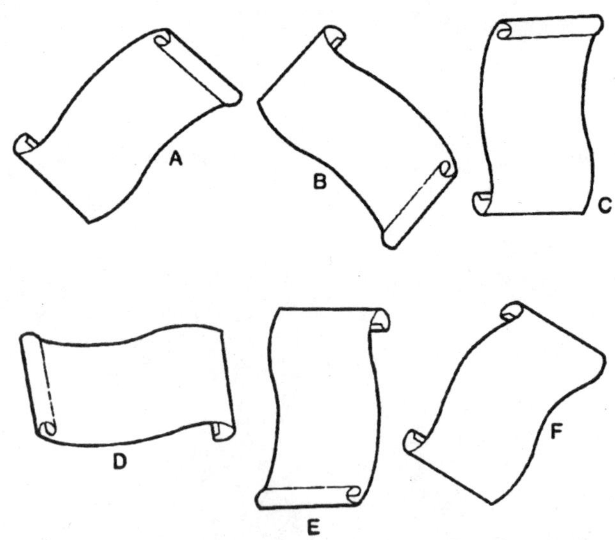

7 Assuming four of these dates are correct, which one is wrong?

(A) SATURDAY, JANUARY 7, 1764
(B) SATURDAY, JANUARY 21, 1764
(C) SATURDAY, FEBRUARY 11, 1764
(D) SATURDAY, MARCH 11, 1764
(E) SATURDAY, APRIL 14, 1764

8 Which is the odd one out?

(A) CONSTABLE
(B) ABATTOIR
(C) REBATE
(D) COMBATANT
(E) EMBATTLED

9 Two three-letter words will go into the brackets to complete two other words. Give both words.

C A (– – –) E T

10 Which gentleman has changed his appearance?

11 What are x and y?

7 8 6 9 5 10 x y

12 Which of these moons are waxing (becoming larger)?

13 Which of the words at the right goes with those at the left?

PASSED	(A) BLUSC
EARTHS	(B) ASSET
DAD SIMON	(C) PALMS
	(D) SPARE

14 Which shield is wrong?

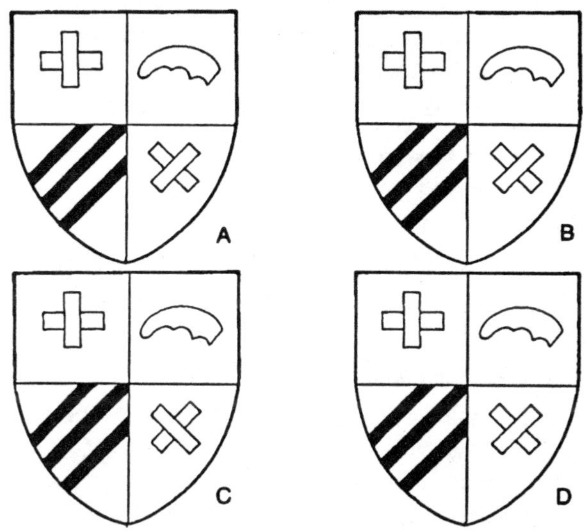

15 Add the difference between the two lowest numbers to the difference between the two highest numbers:

91 13 76 12 7 88 17 84 11
14 87 15 86 16 89 85

NOW CHECK YOUR ANSWERS AND KEEP A NOTE OF YOUR TOTAL SCORE ON PAGE 24.

ANSWERS TO TEST 1

1 (1) (E); (2) (F); (3) (I); (4) (A); (5) (G); (6) (H); (7) (C); (8) (D); (9) (B) **(SCORE 1 IF ALL CORRECT; SCORE ½ POINT IF 8 ARE CORRECT).**

TENNIS can pair only with MATCH, therefore SAFETY must pair with LOCK. SEE can pair only with SAW, therefore SHOP must pair with WORK. TOY can pair only with STORE, so WORK must pair with BENCH. BAND must go with AGE (SAW has already been used). That leaves IRON and HOUSE in the first column and CLAD and HOLD in the second, which means that HOUSE must pair with HOLD and IRON with CLAD.

2 C **(SCORE 1 POINT).**

The middle scrolls do not conform with the others.

3 S 19 **(SCORE 1 POINT IF BOTH ARE CORRECT).**

There are two separate series. The letters advance missing the first two (A to D), then three (D to H) and so on. After M there must be five missing letters, bringing us to S. The numbers advance in the same way.

4 **(SCORE 1 POINT IF ALL ARE CORRECT).**

(A) NORMAN (B) IRIS (C) ANNE
(D) RICHARD

In (A) the letters have been increased by one place in the alphabet, in (B) by two places, in (C) by three places and in (D) by four places.

5 (D) **(SCORE 1 POINT).**

RAND is the unit currency in South Africa. All the others are slang terms for currency:

(A) GRAND – 1,000 dollars
(B) TEN-SPOT – 10 dollars
(C) BUCK – dollar
(D) C-NOTE – 100 dollars
(E) BEN FRANKLIN – 100 dollars
(F) CLAM – dollar
(G) GREENBACK – dollar
(I) FIVER – 5 dollars

6 F **(SCORE 1 POINT).**

Both scrolls are turned the same way; in all the others one is turned inwards and the other outwards.

7 (D) **(SCORE 1 POINT).**

Since 1764 was a leap year, there were 29 days in February, so it would be Saturday, March 10 not March 11.

8 (A) **(SCORE 1 POINT).**

All the other words contain BAT. CONSTABLE contains those letters in reverse order.

9 BIN and BAR **(SCORE 1 POINT IF BOTH ARE CORRECT).**

The words are CABINET and CABARET.

10 F **(SCORE 1 POINT).**

His mustache differs from B and G.

11 x is 4; y is 11 **(SCORE 1 POINT IF BOTH ARE CORRECT).**

There are two alternate series.
One is: 7 6 5 4
The other is: 8 9 10 11

12 A, B and E **(SCORE 1 POINT IF ALL ARE CORRECT).**

With regard to the shape of the moon, D comes before C: when the moon is in the shape of D it is waxing and when in the shape of C it is waning (diminishing in size).

13 (A) **(SCORE 1 POINT).**

This is an anagram of CLUBS, and the three on top are anagrams of the other suits:
PASSED – SPADES; EARTHS – HEARTS;
DAD SIMON – DIAMONDS

14 C **(SCORE 1 POINT).**

The cross in the bottom right quarter is different from those in the other shields.

15 6 **(SCORE 1 POINT).**

Remember to keep a note of your score.

NOTES

1, 4, 7 and 13 caused the most difficulty or took the longest time to solve. Most points were lost on 4 and 13.

However, on the whole the problems in this test were not too difficult. They were deliberately intended to introduce you gently to the types of problems you will encounter later, which will become progressively more difficult.

TEST 2

Time limit: 15 minutes

1 Which is the odd one out?

(A) CHAPEL
(B) PROBING
(C) SCATTER
(D) MILLIONAIRE
(E) PALLBEARER
(F) SHAREHOLDER

2 Assuming that the top two cars are correct, which of those below are wrong?

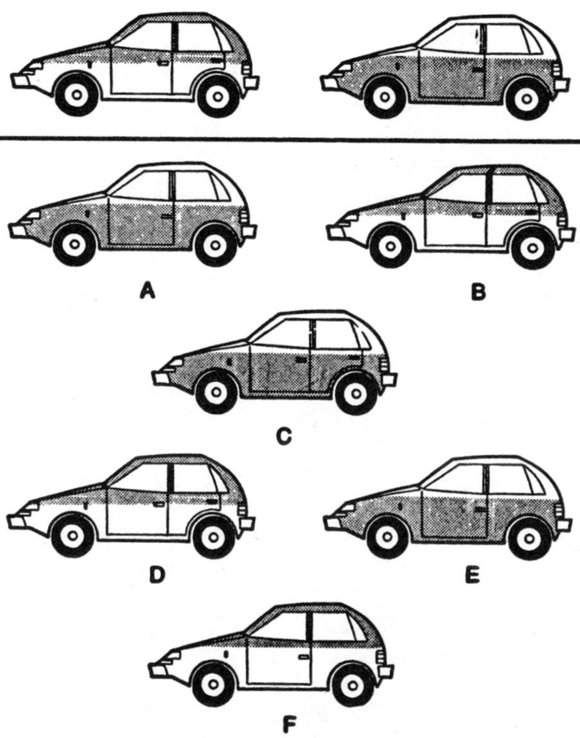

3 What are x and y?

1 3 3 6 5 9 7 12 x y

4 What places are these?

(A) U V S J O
(B) Q B S J T
(C) M P O E P O
(D) C F S M J O

5 What letter completes this word?

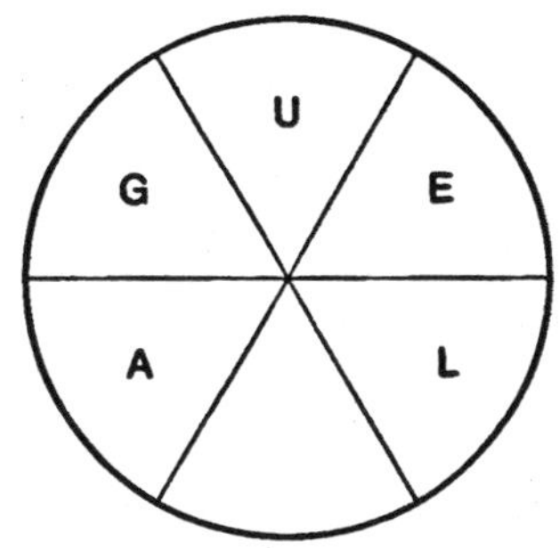

6 Change KNIT into SHOP in four moves, changing one letter at a time.

KNIT
1 – – – –
2 – – – –
3 – – – –
4 SHOP

7 The same three-letter word inside the brackets will complete all these words:

S C (– – –)
B E H (– – –)
H (– – –) A L L
S (– – –) I E R

8 The map above shows the places listed below. Using your eyes only, imagine a line joining Dallas to Minneapolis. Now imagine a line going from Washington D.C. to San Francisco. What city will be nearest to the intersection of these lines?

ATLANTA	MINNEAPOLIS
CHICAGO	NEW YORK
DALLAS	OKLAHOMA CITY
DENVER	PORTLAND
EL PASO	SAN ANTONIO
KANSAS CITY	SAN FRANCISCO
LOS ANGELES	WASHINGTON D.C.

9 Which is the odd one out?

(A) ARTIST
(B) I START
(C) TRAITS
(D) STAIRS
(E) STRAIT
(F) IT'S TAR

10 Which soccer player is incorrectly dressed?

11 Which of these could NOT be drawn with a continuous unbroken line without crossing another line?

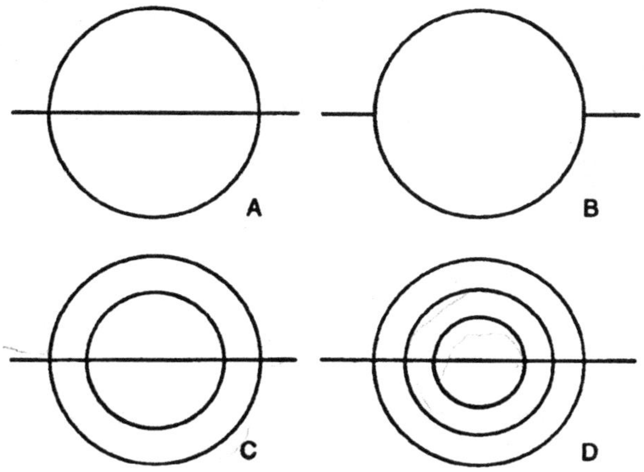

12 Subtract the sum of the three lowest numbers from the sum of the three highest numbers.

11 36 7 38 3 45 39 10 48 37 12 36

13 Two answers are required here.

(A) Can you make sense out of this?

THEM OMEN TOFT RUTH

(B) Can you make sense out of this?

HAL FALO AFIS BET TERT

HAN NOB READ

14 Which word in the second line belongs to the group in the first line?

DOG CAT PIG RABBIT

APE EWE EAGLE ERNE LAMB

15 Group these pictures into four pairs.

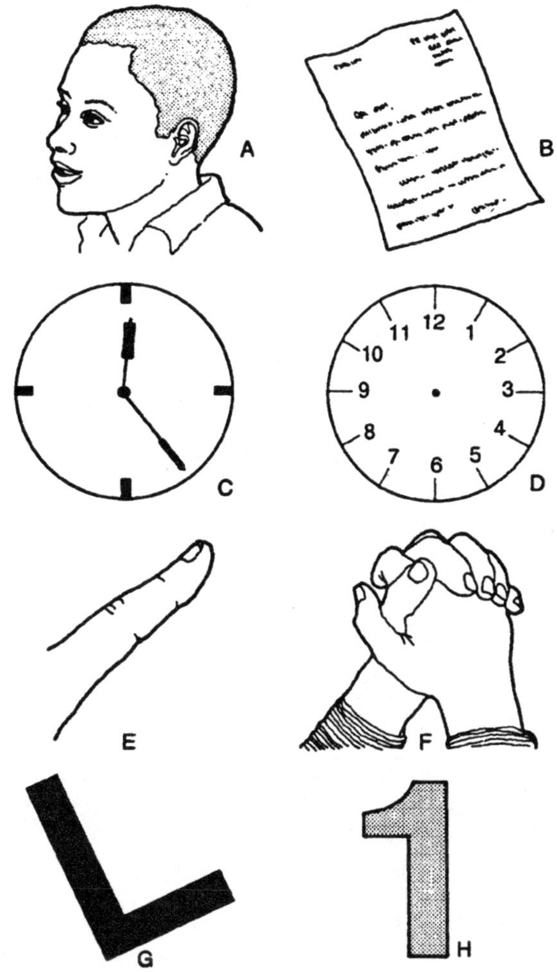

NOW CHECK YOUR ANSWERS AND KEEP A NOTE OF YOUR TOTAL SCORE ON PAGE 24.

ANSWERS TO TEST 2

1 (B) **(SCORE 1 POINT).**

This word contains a bird – ROBIN. All the others contain animals:

(A) APE (C) CAT (D) LION (E) BEAR (F) HARE

2 C and F **(SCORE 1 POINT IF BOTH ARE CORRECT).**

3 x is 9; y is 15 **(SCORE 1 POINT IF BOTH ARE CORRECT).**

There are two separate series. Starting with the first number and taking the others alternately:

1 3 5 7 9

Starting with the second number and proceeding the same way:

3 6 9 12 15

4 **(SCORE 1 POINT IF ALL ARE CORRECT).**

(A) TURIN (B) PARIS (C) LONDON (D) BERLIN

Each letter is reduced by one in the alphabet.

5 E **(SCORE 1 POINT).**

The word is LEAGUE.

6 KNIT; 1 SNIT; 2 SNIP; 3 SHIP; 4 SHOP **(SCORE 1 POINT).**

(You may have used other words, but you still score one point provided they are actual words.)

7 OLD **(SCORE 1 POINT).**

The words are: SCOLD; BEHOLD; HOLDALL; SOLDIER.

8 KANSAS CITY **(SCORE 1 POINT).**

9 (D) **(SCORE 1 POINT).**

All the others are anagrams of ARTIST.

10 E **(SCORE 1 POINT).**

Soccer players in black short wear black socks; those in white shorts wear white socks. E is wearing black shorts and white socks.

11 B **(SCORE 1 POINT).**

As can be seen below, all the others can be drawn with a continuous unbroken line:

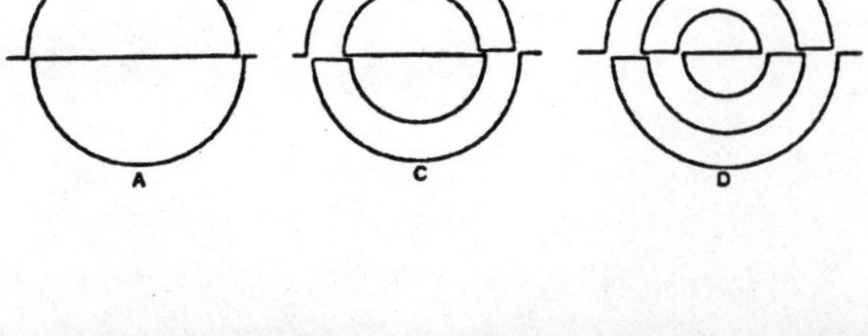

12 112 **(SCORE 1 POINT).**

13 **(SCORE 1 POINT IF BOTH ARE CORRECT.)**

(A) THE MOMENT OF TRUTH

(B) HALF A LOAF IS BETTER THAN NO BREAD

14 LAMB **(SCORE 1 POINT).**

All the words in the first line begin and end with a consonant. In the second line all the words begin and end with a vowel—except LAMB.

15 A D; B G; C F; E H **(SCORE 1 POINT IF ALL CORRECT).**

The pairs are the same words with different connotations:

FACE (human) – clock FACE
LETTER (communication) – LETTER (alphabet)
HANDS (clock) – HANDS (human)
DIGIT (human) – DIGIT (numerical)

Remember to keep a note of your score.

NOTES

None of the problems should have held you up for very long, as little writing was involved.

4 and 8 caused the longest delay. In 2 'are wrong' told you that more than one was wrong, whereas in 10 'is incorrect' told you that only one was wrong.

The best clue in 7 was provided by B E H (– – –), since the only six-letter words which begin with these letters are: BEHALF, BEHAVE, BEHEAD, BEHELD, BEHEST, BEHIND, BEHOLD, BEHOOF and BEHOVE. Obviously, ALF, AVE, EAD, ELD, EST, IND, OOF and OVE will not fit the other words. The only one that is common to all is OLD.

TEST 3

Time limit: 15 minutes

1 Which is the odd one out?

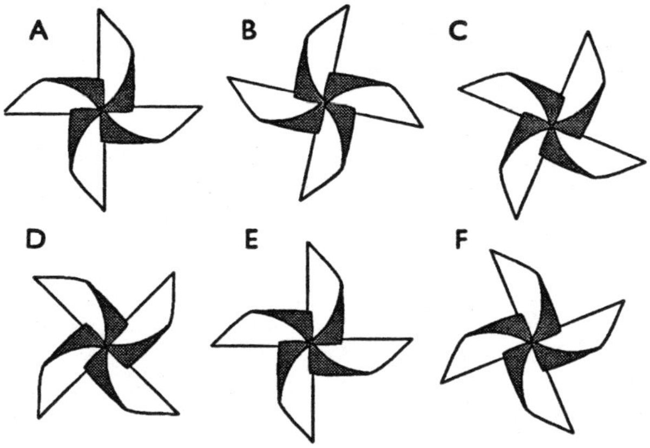

2 What is the last term in this series?

B 2 T G 7 C –

3 What one word can be added to each letter to form the words for which definitions are given?

(A) C	Unfledged
(B) F	Uncultivated
(C) H	Honor as sacred
(D) M	Plant
(E) S	Pale brown
(F) T	Grease
(G) W	Roll about

4 What comes next?

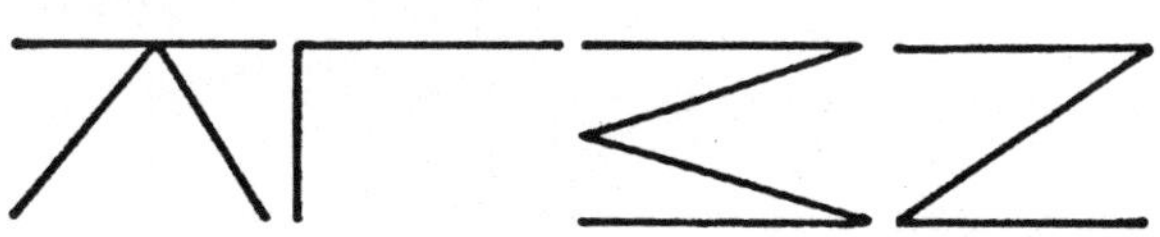

5 What is x?

4 9 x 25

6 Whose face is wrong?

7 What WORD should take the place of x?

W x F S S

8 Give words that will fit each definition.

(A) Part of the body – Coffer
(B) Theater seat – Play for time
(C) Aircraft – Carpenter's tool
(D) Precious stones – Suit
(E) Animal part – Target
(F) Herb – Naïve
(G) Cultivate – Groom
(H) Horny growth – Grain
(I) Dance – Sphere
(J) Game – Metal rod

9 Which one is wrong?

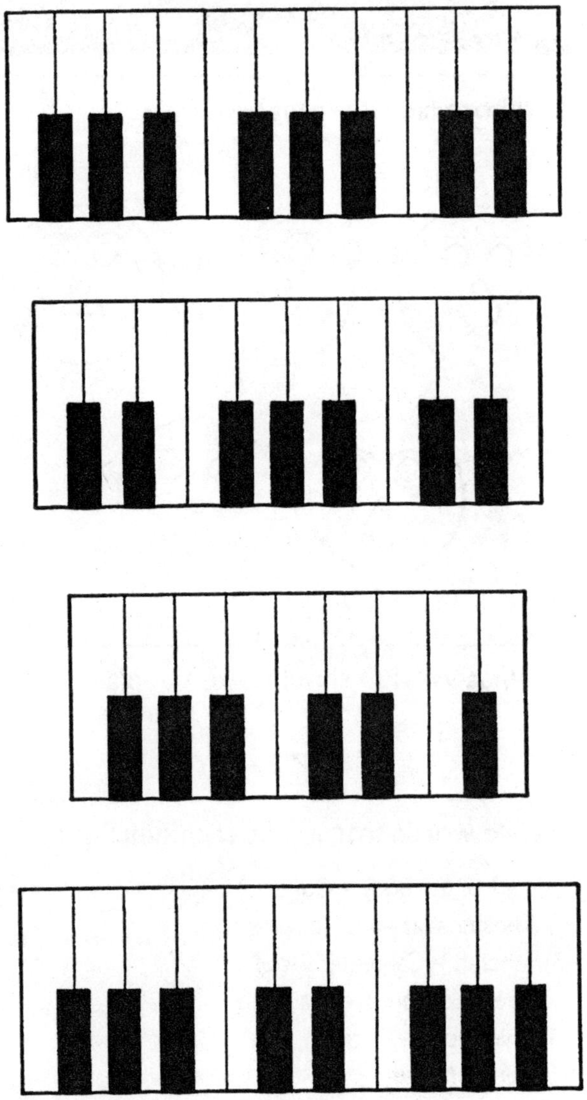

10 What comes next?

208 CIV 52 XXVI –

11 Which one does not conform with the others?

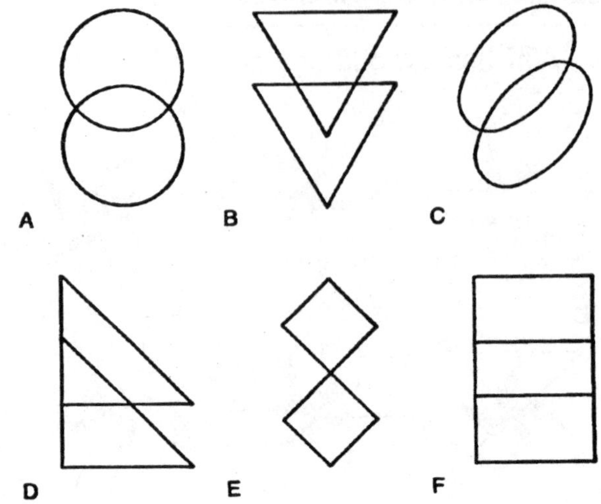

12 Find the words that go into the brackets. Each one must logically follow the previous word and precede the next: e.g. SAFETY (CURTAIN) RAISER.

ELASTIC
(   )
MASTER
(   )
WORK
(   )
WINDOW
(   )
TABLE
(   )
GLASS

13 Which knot is different?

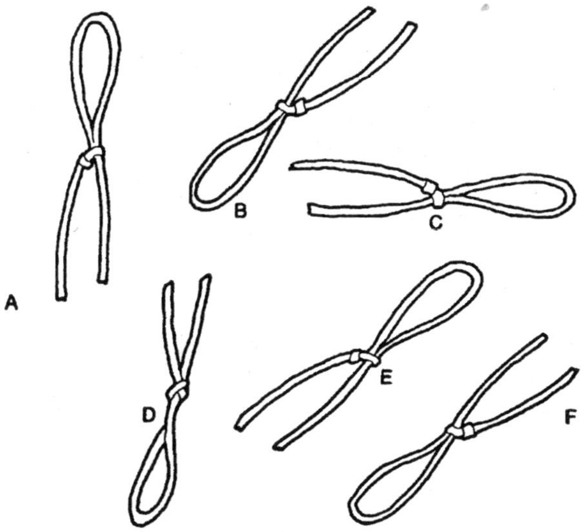

14 What letter completes the word?

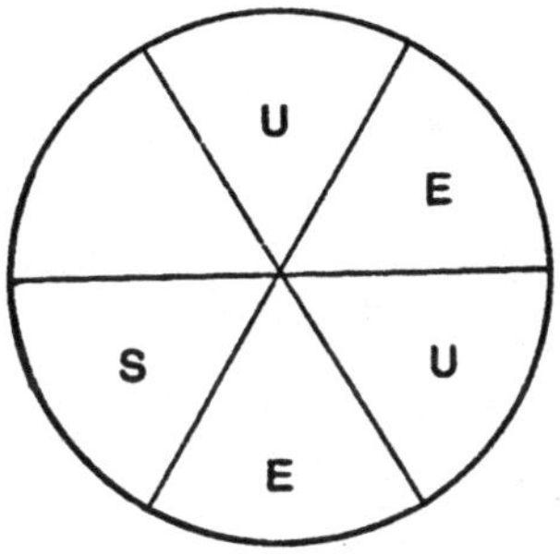

15 Which date does not conform with the others?

(A) 1417 (B) 1533 (C) 1605 (D) 1722
(E) 1812 (F) 1902

NOW CHECK YOUR ANSWERS AND KEEP A NOTE OF YOUR SCORE ON PAGE 24.

ANSWERS TO TEST 3

1 B **(SCORE 1 POINT).**

2 3 **(SCORE 1 POINT).**

The numbers following the letters correspond with the position in the alphabet of the letters.

3 ALLOW **(SCORE 1 POINT).**

The words are: (A) CALLOW; (B) FALLOW; (C) HALLOW; (D) MALLOW; (E) SALLOW; (F) TALLOW; (G) WALLOW

4 O **(SCORE 1 POINT).**

The letters K L M N have been turned on their sides. O is the next letter.

5 16 **(SCORE 1 POINT).**

4 is the square of 2; 9 is the square of 3; 25 is the square of 5; x must be the square of 4 (16).

6 B **(SCORE 1 POINT).**

The face in B is composed of three circles, four straight lines and five curves. All the other faces have four circles, four straight lines and four curves.

7 THURSDAY **(SCORE 1 POINT).**

Obviously they are the days of the week:

W Wednesday
T Thursday (x)
F Friday
S Saturday
S Sunday

(Note: T alone is not acceptable, as the question asks what WORD should take the place of x.)

8 **(SCORE 1 POINT IF ALL CORRECT; ½ IF 8 OR 9.)**

(A) CHEST; (B) STALL; (C) PLANE; (D) DIAMONDS; (E) BULLSEYE; (F) SIMPLE (G) HUSBAND; (H) CORN; (I) BALL; (J) POKER

9 A **(SCORE 1 POINT).**

These are the keys of a piano. It is not possible to have two groups of three black keys next to each other.

10 13 **(SCORE 1 POINT).**

Change the Roman numerals into modern numbers:

208 104 52 26

Each one is half the previous number. Therefore the next number is 13, expressed in modern numerals to conform with the established pattern.

11 E **(SCORE 1 POINT).**

In all the others identical shapes overlap:

(A) two circles
(B) two equilateral triangles
(C) two ovals
(D) two right-angled triangles
(F) two squares

In E there are two diamonds which do not overlap.

12 **(SCORE 1 POINT IF ALL ARE CORRECT.)**

BAND
PIECE
SHOP
DRESSING
WINE

13 D **(SCORE 1 POINT).**

14 Q **(SCORE 1 POINT).**

The word is QUEUES.

15 (A) **(SCORE 1 POINT).**

With the exception of the digits in (A), which add up to 13, the digits in all the other dates add up to 12.

Remember to keep a note of your score.

NOTES

No great difficulties in this test, but the limited time allowance was a drawback for slow thinkers.

A few of the volunteers were caught by 7, failing to recognize that the letters were the initials of the days of the week. Because of the short time allowed, few succeeded in scoring maximum points in 8. In 11 it was easy to choose F, believing it to be a rectangle touching a square, when in fact it shows two overlapping squares. In 12 TABLE WINE seemed to be the biggest stumbling-block. The unusual letters in 14 defeated many. Because of the sort time allowance, even going right through the alphabet to arrive at the answer often did not meet the bill, as Q comes so late in the succession.

Without doubt, most would have scored maximum points had there not been time constraints, which were deliberately imposed to compensate for the comparative simplicity of the problems.

TEST 4

Time limit: 25 minutes

1 Pair words in the first column with words in the second column, finishing with ten related pairs.

(A) MIDDLE	(1) COAT
(B) OLYMPIC	(2) FATHER
(C) BULL	(3) GO
(D) TURN	(4) GROUND
(E) OVER	(5) LADDER
(F) UNDER	(6) AROUND
(G) FOR	(7) STILE
(H) OUT	(8) STAND
(I) GRAND	(9) BID
(J) STEP	(10) GAMES

2 Which one is wrong?

(A) 9/4 + 1.75 = 4
(B) 9/5 + 2.2 = 4
(C) 6/5 + 2.8 = 4
(D) 6/4 + 1.5 = 4
(E) 9/6 + 2.5 = 4

3 Arrange these zodiac signs in their relative pairs.

(1) ARIES	(A) WATER CARRIER
(2) CANCER	(B) ARCHER
(3) AQUARIUS	(C) CRAB
(4) LIBRA	(D) FISHES
(5) PISCES	(E) RAM
(6) SAGITTARIUS	(F) SCALES

4 Arrange these into five pairs.

A

B

C

D

E
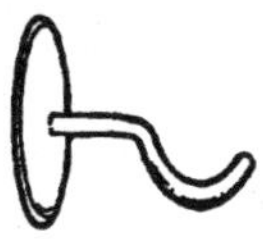

F

G
9

H

I
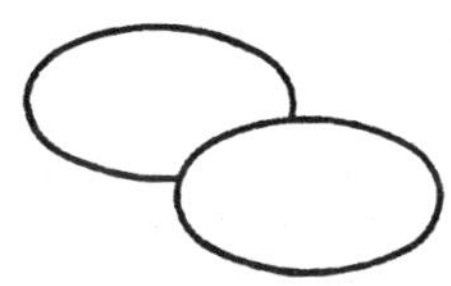

J

5 Words are often associated in pairs, such as 'ducks and drakes'. Complete these pairs:

(A) CHAPTER and—
(B) —and READY
(C) HALE and—
(D) VIM and—
(E) —and ENDS
(F) CUT and—
(G) HIT and—
(H) —and FURIOUS
(I) —and PARCEL
(J) BAG and—

6 What is x?

1 2 4 8 1 6 3 2 6 x

7 WITHOUT REFERRING, whose picture appears on one side of a half dollar coin?

8 Multiply the second highest number by the second lowest number and then divide the result by the third lowest number.

10 35 2 32 37 33 9
13 36 12 14 34 3 11

9 What is x?

3 6 10 15 x 28

10 What comes next?

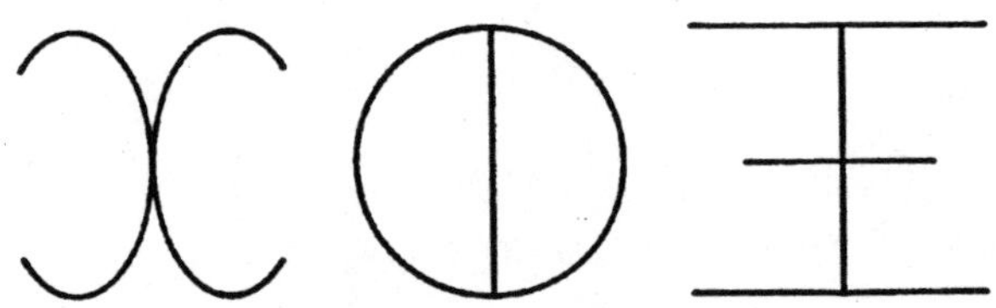

11 Which is the odd one out?

(A) TOMATO
(B) CABBAGE
(C) POTATO
(D) LEEK
(E) CARROT

12 Which of the circles at the bottom should take the place of No. 2 at the top?

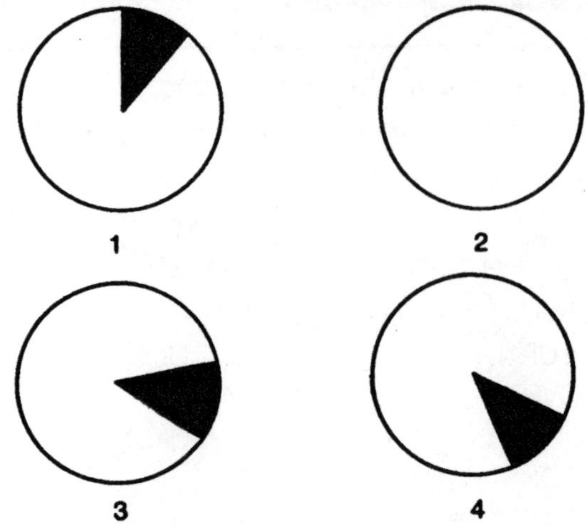

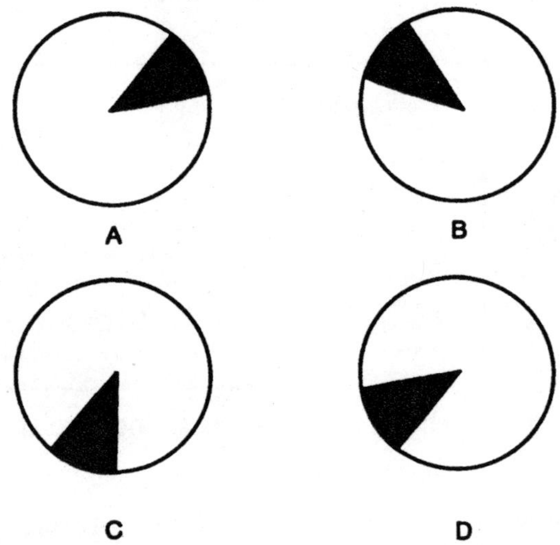

13 If the two figures at the top are correct, which of those below are wrong?

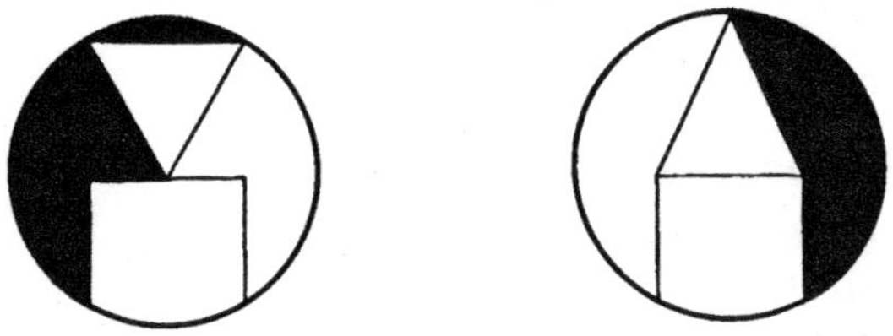

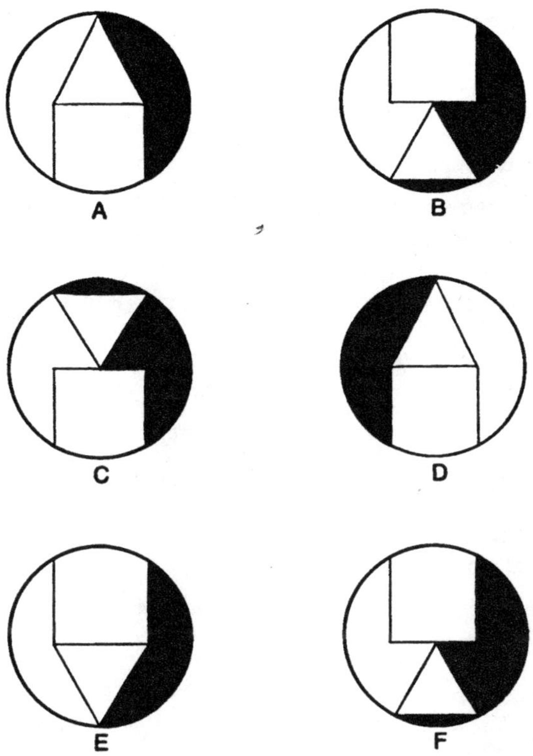

14 Two different letters placed in the empty segment will form two different words. Give both letters.

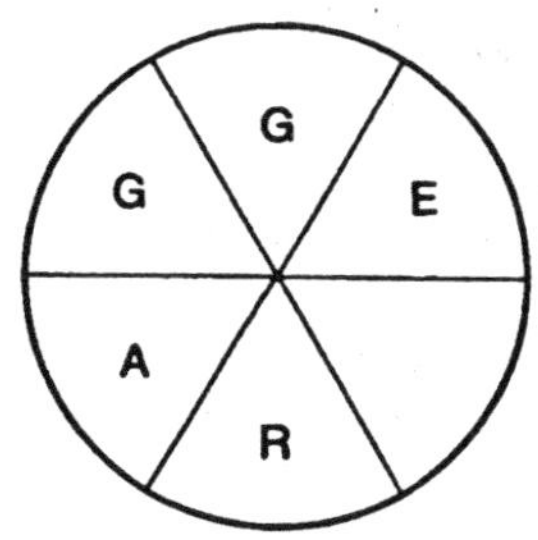

15 Which one is wrong?

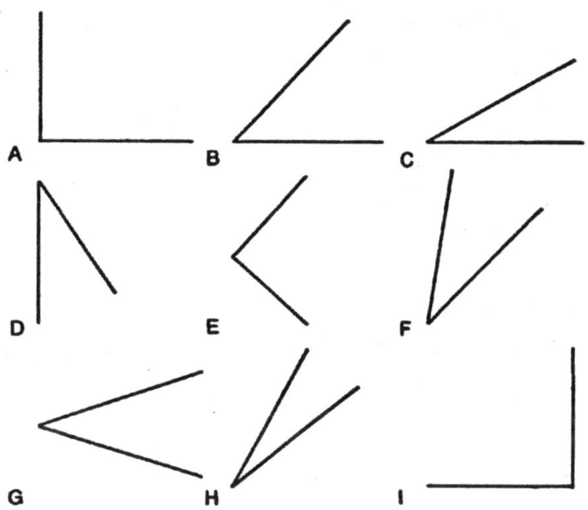

NOW CHECK YOUR ANSWERS AND KEEP A NOTE OF YOUR SCORE ON PAGE 24.

ANSWERS TO TEST 4

1 (A) (4); (B) (10); (C) (6); (D) (7); (E) (1); (F) (8); (G) (3); (H) (9); (I) (2); (J) (5)
(SCORE 1 POINT IF ALL ARE CORRECT; ½ IF 8 OR 9.)

2 (D) **(SCORE 1 POINT).**

(D) equals 3; all the others equal 4.

3 (SCORE 1 POINT IF ALL ARE CORRECT).
(1) (E); (2) (C); (3) (A); (4) (F); (5) (D); (6) (B)

4 (SCORE 1 POINT IF ALL ARE CORRECT.)
Rhyming pairs:

A	(ACE)	J	(FACE)
B	(BOOK)	E	(HOOK)
C	(LINE)	G	(NINE)
D	(PAN)	H	(CAN)
F	(LEGS)	I	(EGGS)

5 (SCORE 1 POINT IF ALL ARE CORRECT; ½ IF 8 OR 9.)
(A) VERSE; (B) ROUGH; (C) HALE; (D) VIM; (E) ODDS; (F) DRIED (or THRUST); (G) RUN; (H) FAST; (I) PART; (J) BAGGAGE

6 4 **(SCORE 1 POINT).**
The series is incorrectly spaced. When corrected it reads:
1 2 4 8 16 32 64

7 John F. Kennedy **(SCORE 1 POINT).**

8 12 **(SCORE 1 POINT).**

9 21 **(SCORE 1 POINT).**
The numbers increase by 3, 4, 5, 6 and 7.

10 (SCORE 1 POINT).

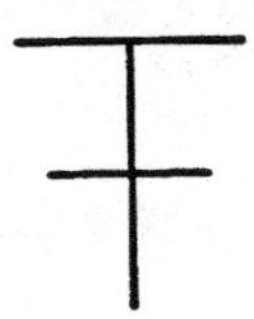

The letters are C, D and E. In each case they are paired and joined together, first reversed and then printed correctly. The next letter is F, arranged in the same way.

11 (A) **(SCORE 1 POINT).**
TOMATO is a fruit. All the others are vegetables.

12 A **(SCORE 1 POINT).**
The black section rotates clockwise 40° at a time.

13 C, D, E **(SCORE 1 POINT IF ALL ARE CORRECT).**

14 D and B **(SCORE 1 POINT IF BOTH ARE CORRECT).**

The words are RAGGED and BEGGAR.

15 G **(SCORE 1 POINT).**
The angle is 60°. The others are 90°, 45° or 30°.

Keep a note of your score.

NOW TOTAL UP YOUR SCORES FOR THE FIRST FOUR TESTS.

NOTES

There were no great difficulties in this test.

14 gave some trouble: although RAGGED stood out fairly prominently, BEGGAR was not so obvious.

RATINGS AND IQ SCORES FOR GROUP I

TEST I	Average 10 points
TEST II	Average 9 points
TEST III	Average 9 ½ points
TEST IV	Average 9 points

TOTAL FOR THE GROUP
(Out of a possible 60 points)

Over 54	Excellent
42–54	Very Good
38–41	Good
37½	Average
30–37	Fair
Under 30	Poor

YOUR SCORES FOR ELEMENTARY TESTS

TEST 1	______
TEST 2	______
TEST 3	______
TEST 4	______
TOTAL	______

SEE IQ SCORING INSTRUCTIONS ON PAGE 63

GROUP II

CHALLENGING

TEST 1

Time limit: 40 minutes

1 **Which anagram is the odd one out?**

(A) REDRESS
(B) BLEAT
(C) BROADSIDE
(D) GARDEN
(E) LOOTS

2 **Which tumbler is wrong?**

3 **From a certain station a northbound train ran every ten minutes throughout the day; a southbound train also ran every ten minutes throughout the day. A man went to the station every day at random times and caught the first train that arrived. On average he caught the northbound train nine times out of ten. Why was this?**

4 **What is x?**

3	4	13
8	8	56
1	5	24
9	7	40
2	2	2
6	4	10
7	5	18
4	9	77
5	3	X

5 **Which is the odd word out?**

(A) MICA
(B) ACRE
(C) SOLD
(D) TOMB
(E) TIED
(F) UPON

6 **And which is the odd one out here?**

(A) GAMMA
(B) KAPPA
(C) IOTA
(D) NAFTA
(E) OMEGA
(F) ETA

7 **If ELK/GNU = $\frac{2}{3}$ and HEN/FOX = $\frac{3}{5}$, what is this?**

PIG/RAM

8 Pair the words in the first column with the words in the second column, finishing with ten related pairs.

(A) STONE	(1) DAY
(B) FREE	(2) MOON
(C) HARVEST	(3) WALL
(D) MONUMENTAL	(4) HAND
(E) CORN	(5) FALL
(F) HALF	(6) FESTIVAL
(G) RIGHT	(7) HEARTED
(H) SECOND	(8) STONE
(I) SUN	(9) MINDED
(J) BIG	(10) FLOWER

9 What are x, y and z?

76 69 52 65 60 45 54 51 38
43 42 31 32 33 24 X Y Z

10 What are x and y?

S	20
8	J
W	25
16	T
A	4
5	K
C	7
x	L
A	y
4	N

11 Which of the figures at the bottom should come next?

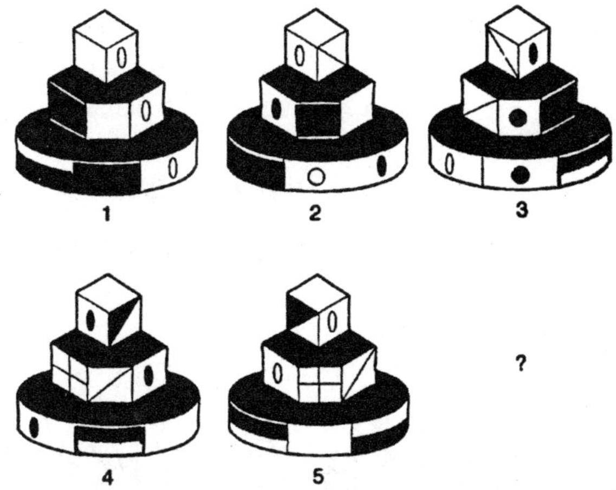

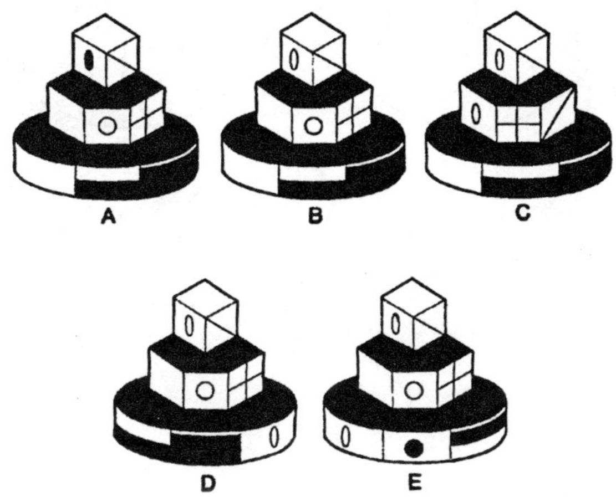

12 A rotates clockwise all the time, one position at a time. If it stops on an odd number, ball B moves one place counterclockwise; if A stops on an even number, B moves three places clockwise. If ball B stops on an even number, ball C moves three places clockwise; if B stops on an odd number, C moves five places counterclockwise.

At the end of six moves what place will be spelled out by ball C?

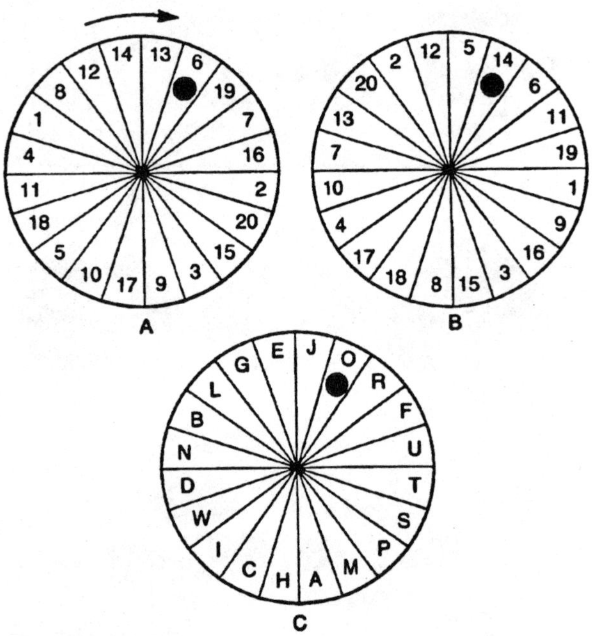

13 What time will this clock show in 3½ hours' time, assuming that it loses four seconds in every hour? (State the exact time.)

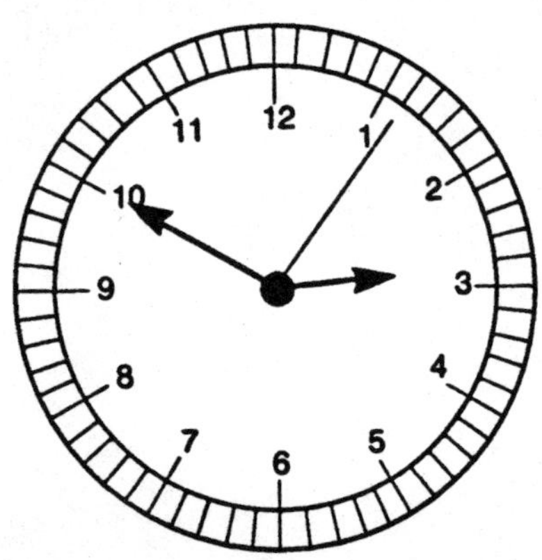

14 A turns clockwise, two positions at a time. B turns counterclockwise, three positions at a time. After six moves, what will be the total of the two front faces? (The concealed numbers progress in the same way as the visible numbers: 7, 9 and 11 on A and 8, 10, 12 on B.)

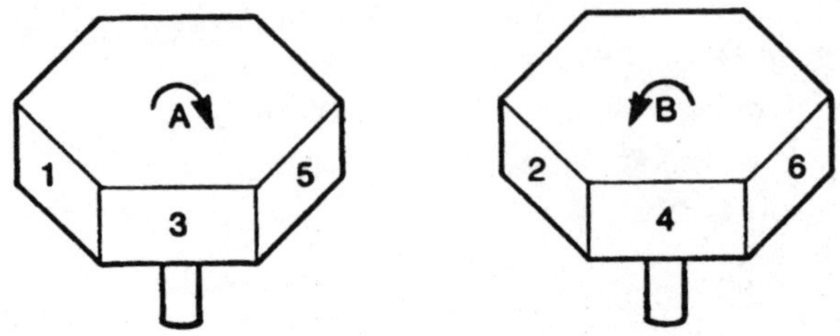

15 Assuming that the top two houses are correct, which of those below are wrong?

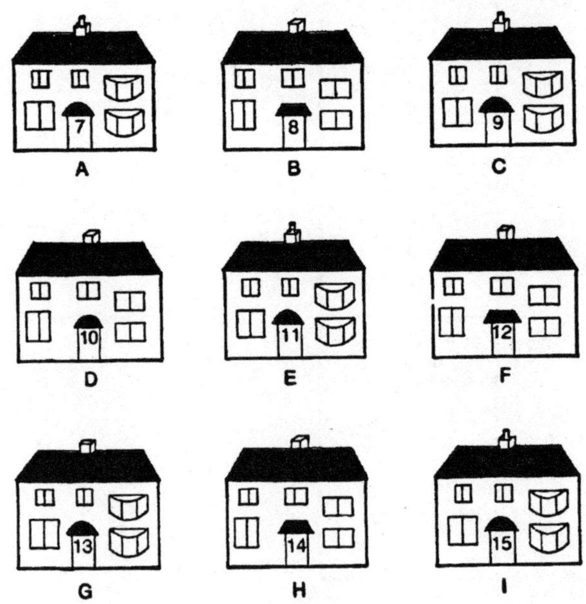

ANSWERS TO TEST 1

1 (D) (SCORE 1 POINT).

All except (D) are anagrams of furniture:

(A) REDRESS – DRESSER
(B) BLEAT – TABLE
(C) BROADSIDE – SIDEBOARD
(D) LOOTS – STOOL

2 F (SCORE 1 POINT).

The design around the top should consist entirely of diamond shapes, as in B and L. One of the diamonds has become a square.

3 The southbound train ran one minute after the northbound train (SCORE 1 POINT).

4 x is 4 (SCORE 1 POINT).

Square the middle number in each horizontal row and subtract the left-hand number to give the right-hand number. So, in the bottom row:

3 squared is	9
Subtract	5
x is	4

5 (B) (SCORE 1 POINT).

All others are made up with letters in reverse alphabetical order:

(A) MICA – ACIM
(C) SOLD – DLOS
(D) TOMB – BMOT
(E) TIED – DEIT
(F) UPON – NOPU

6 (D) (SCORE 1 POINT).

NAFTA is the acronym for the North American Free Trade Agreement. The others are letters in the Greek alphabet.

(A) GAMMA – the third letter in the Greek alphabet
(B) KAPPA – the Greek letter k
(C) IOTA – the Greek letter i
(E) OMEGA – the last letter (Ω) in the Greek alphabet (hence 'alpha to omega')
(F) ETA – the Greek letter η

7 1 (SCORE 1 POINT).

Give each letter a value according to its position in the alphabet:

$$\frac{\text{ELK}}{\text{GNU}} = \frac{5\quad 12\quad 11}{7\quad 14\quad 21}$$

$$\frac{\text{HEN}}{\text{FOX}} = \frac{8\quad 5\quad 14}{6\quad 15\quad 24}$$

$$\frac{\text{PIG}}{\text{RAM}} = \frac{16\quad 9\quad 7}{18\quad 1\quad 13}$$

Add the numbers:

$$\frac{28}{42} \qquad \frac{27}{45} \qquad \frac{32}{32}$$

Which gives us:

$\frac{4}{6}$ or $\frac{2}{3}$ $\qquad \frac{3}{5} \qquad \frac{1}{1}$ (which gives the answer 1)

8 (A) (3); (B) (5); (C) (6); (D) (8); (E) (10); (F) (2); (G) (9); (H) (4); (I) (1); (J) (7) **(SCORE 1 POINT IF ALL ARE CORRECT; ½ IF 8 OR 9).**

9 x is 21; y is 24; z is 17 (SCORE 1 POINT IF ALL ARE CORRECT).

There are three separate series. Start with the first term and take every third term thereafter:

76 65 54 43 32

As they reduce by 11 each time, the next term (x) must be 21. From the second term, proceed in the same way:

69 60 51 42 33

These reduce by 9 each time, so the next term (y) is 24. From the third term, proceed in the same way:

52 45 38 31 24

As they reduce by 7 each time the next term (z) is 17.

10 x is 4; y is 6 (SCORE 1 POINT IF BOTH ARE CORRECT).

Expressing each letter as a number according to position in the alphabet, the table appears as below, with what were originally letters circled:

19	20
8	10
23	25
16	20
1	4
5	11
3	7
x	12
1	y
4	14

11 B **(SCORE 1 POINT).**

The cube rotates clockwise; the hexagon rotates counterclockwise; the circle rotates clockwise.

12 BERLIN **(SCORE 1 POINT).**

The moves are as follows:

	BALL A	BALL B	BALL C
1st move	19	5	B
2nd move	7	12	E
3rd move	16	6	R
4th move	2	1	L
5th move	20	3	I
6th move	15	16	N

13 **6 hours, 19 minutes, 52 seconds (SCORE 1 POINT).**

The present time shown is 2 hours, 50 minutes, 6 seconds. Ignoring the seconds, the time in 3½ hours will be 6:20. In the meantime, the second hand will have lost 14 seconds. Instead of showing six seconds after the hour it will show eight seconds BEFORE the hour—that is, 52 seconds. This means that the minute hand will not have reached the 20-minute mark, but will have passed the 19-minute mark.

14 7 **(SCORE 1 POINT).**

The moves result as follows:

	A	B	
1st move	7	10	
2nd move	11	4	
3rd move	3	10	
4th move	7	4	
5th move	11	10	
6th move	3	4	(Total: 7)

15 D and G **(SCORE 1 POINT IF BOTH ARE CORRECT; ½ IF ONE).**

D (a house with an even number) should have a flat porch. G (a house with an odd number) should have a chimney stack.

REMEMBER TO KEEP A NOTE OF YOUR SCORE ON PAGE 45.

NOTES

This test called for quick and clear thinking, and it is extremely unlikely that you completed all the questions within the time limit—deliberately chosen to encourage quick thinking. Because of this, and the difficult nature of the problems, inevitably low averages were recorded by the test group volunteers.

To obtain maximum points it is best to go fairly quickly through all the questions and at first answer only those which seem quite easy or quick to solve. Then you can return to those that were more difficult or would obviously have taken much longer, especially if a considerable amount of writing was necessary.

In this test 3, 7, 8, 12, 13 and 14 would have taken longest either to solve or to write down. It would have been a good idea to have left them while you worked on the others first. To have dwelt too long on any of the extra difficult ones could have deprived you of valuable time, leaving you with less time to spend on the easier problems. Remember, those six problems could have gained only six points (and that is assuming you solved them all correctly). In spending this time on them you may have sacrificed anything up to 9 points on problems which you could have solved, given time to do so.

In comparison with the tests in Group 1, you must have found this one much more difficult, though it is hoped that the experience you gain working on these tests will gradually give you a greater understanding of them.

TEST 2

Time limit: 50 minutes (After 25 minutes, take a break and then resume for the next 25 minutes)

1 If CROCUS is 7, LUPIN is 12 and ROSE is 17, what is TULIP?

2 Which of the designs at the bottom should occupy the empty space?

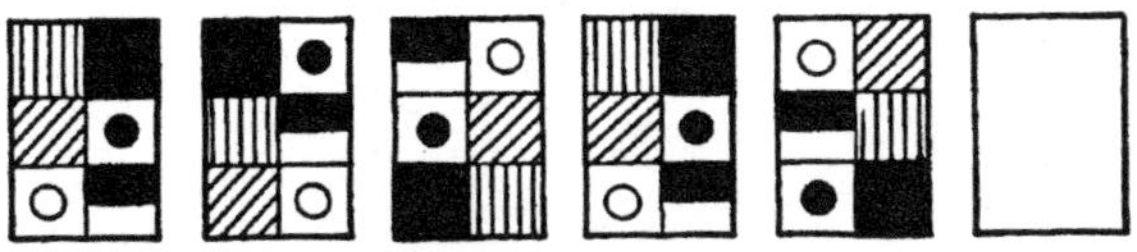

3 What comes next in this series?

625 1296 25 365 –

4 Study the top cards and find what city is represented by the bottom cards.

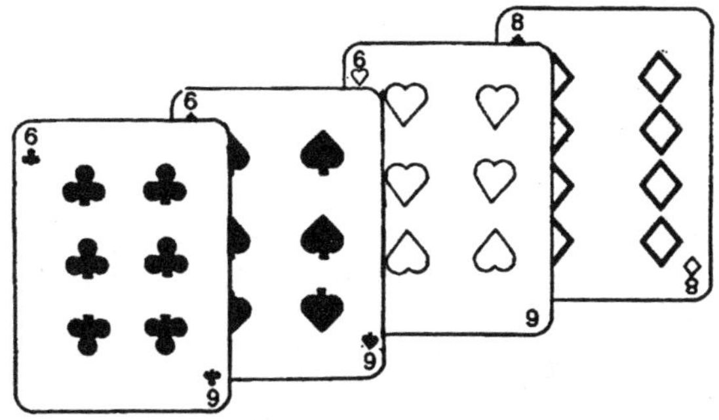

5 Find one word to fit the first definition and then, change one letter to make the word fit the second definition.

(A) Tell – Physically weak through age
(B) Settle – Laugh to scorn
(C) Month – Rightly
(D) Season ticket holder – Calculating machine
(E) Oval – Outshine
(F) Silent – Bed covering
(G) Corrupt – Holy man
(H) Emperor – It means nothing

6 What goes into the empty brackets?

144 (3625) 125
96 (1618) 126
112 ( ) 144

---

7 What are x, y and z?

CIFE	HFGB	GECH
BFEA	CIED	CABD
FFAF	ABFBF	x y z 4

---

8 Two poets are mixed up in each of these:

(A) DRY NORTH-WEST NOW, SON.
(B) DAFT LIMEHOUSE? YES!
(C) A LEVEL C.O. SO HUMAN!

---

9 Which of those at the bottom comes next?

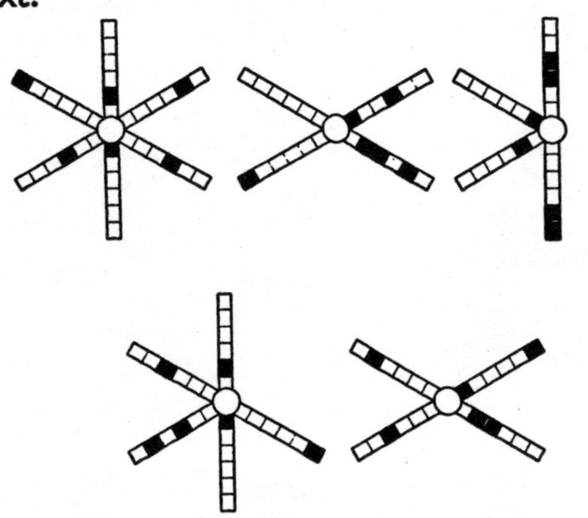

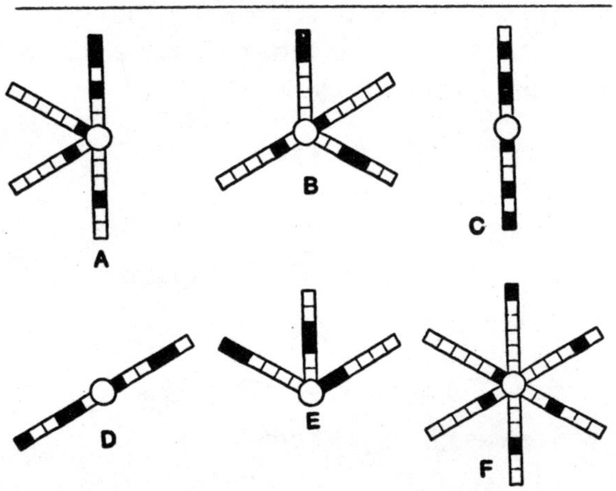

---

10 What is the last term in the bottom line?

⅕	.4	⅗	.8	1
⅓	1	1⅔	2.33	3
¼	1	1¾	2.5	3¼
⅛	.625	1⅛	1.625	—

---

11 If NAZY equals WEM, FLX equals KE and HVW equals YAK, which of the sequences below equals AZVN?

(A) TEX
(B) HLF
(C) KWE
(D) NYZ
(E) FLE

---

12 What is x?

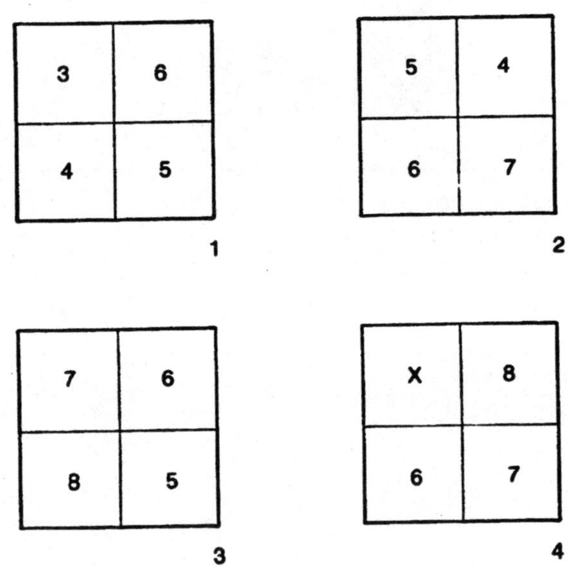

13 Write pairs of words for the definitions given below. In each pair the words are spelled differently but pronounced the same:

(A) SWAN	(1) SEAL
(B) SMALL ISLAND	(2) SMALL HOLE
(C) DINED	(3) NUMBER
(D) DARK PERIOD	(4) CHESS PIECE
(E) CIRCLET	(5) SQUEEZE
(F) EGYPTIAN RULER	(6) CARD GAME
(G) MAN	(7) POST
(H) HIDING-PLACE	(8) MONEY
(I) MAXIMUM HEIGHT	(9) FIXING
(J) VEND	(10) STALL

14 What should go into the empty brackets?

305	(6165)	13
280	(5670)	14
145	(2925)	5
70	(1415)	3
25	( )	1

15 If PEACE is 30, what letter will complete this word and give the same total?

HEA–

NOW CHECK YOUR ANSWERS AND KEEP A NOTE OF YOUR SCORE ON PAGE 45.

ANSWERS TO TEST 2

1 18 (SCORE 1 POINT).

Give each letter a value according to its position in the alphabet. Add the total of the consonants in each word and subtract the total of the value of the vowels:

T	20	U	21
L	12	I	9
P	16		30
	48		

30 subtracted from 48 gives the answer: 18.

2 D (SCORE 1 POINT).

The black square moves counterclockwise, first one position, then two, then three, and so on. All other squares move in the same way.

3 6 (SCORE 1 POINT).

There are two separate series here. Starting with the first term and taking alternate terms thereafter:

625 25 5

Each term is the square root of the previous term Starting with the second term:

1296 36 6

Again, each term is the square root of the previous number.

4 MOSCOW (SCORE 1 POINT).

This problem is based on the fact that 26 cards make half of a full deck of playing cards, and there are also 26 letters in the alphabet. These 26 letters are represented by the cards at the top:

Clubs	Ace to 6	A to F
Spades	Ace to 6	G to L
Hearts	Ace to 6	M to R
Diamonds	Ace to 8	S to Z

Thus the cards at bottom are:

Ace of hearts	13th letter	M
3 of hearts	15th letter	O
Ace of diamonds	19th letter	S
3 of clubs	3rd letter	C
3 of hearts	15th letter	O
5 of diamonds	23rd letter	W

5 (SCORE 1 POINT IF ALL ARE CORRECT; ½ IF 7.)

(A) INFORM – INFIRM
(B) DECIDE – DERIDE
(C) JULY – DULY
(D) COMMUTER – COMPUTER
(E) ELLIPSE – ECLIPSE
(F) QUIET – QUILT
(G) TAINT – SAINT
(H) NERO – ZERO

6 1416 (SCORE 1 POINT).

In the first line divide the number on the left by 4 and the number on the right by 5, placing the results inside the brackets. In the second line divide the number on the left by 6 and the number on the right by 7, placing the results inside the brackets. Following this procedure, in the third line divide the number on the left by 8 (14) and the number on the right by 9 (16), placing the results inside the brackets (1416).

7 x is 4; y is 4; z is 1 (SCORE 1 POINT IF ALL ARE CORRECT).

Substitute numbers for letters according to the positions of the letters in the alphabet:

C I F E	3 9 6 5
B F E A	2 6 5 1
F F A F	6 6 1 6 (added)
H F G B	8 6 7 2
C I E D	3 9 5 4
A B F B F	1 2 6 2 6 (added)

It is obvious that the last one must be a subtraction because if H (8) were added to D (4) the result would be 2 in the units, whereas 4 is already given:

G E C H	7 5 3 8
C A B D	3 1 2 4
	4 4 1 4 (subtracted)

8 (SCORE 1 POINT IF ALL ARE CORRECT; ½ IF 2.)

(A) TENNYSON and WORDSWORTH
(B) MASEFIELD and SOUTHEY
(C) HOUSMAN and LOVELACE

9 A (SCORE 1 POINT).

From an examination of the black stripes on the vanes, the following facts emerge:

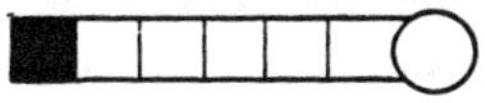
rotates counterclockwise one position at a time

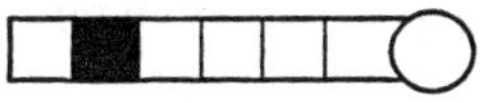
rotates clockwise one position at a time

rotates counterclockwise one position at a time

rotates counterclockwise two positions at a time

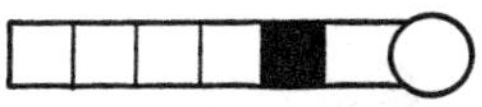
rotates clockwise two positions at a time

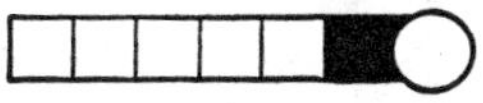
rotates counterclockwise two positions at a time

10 $2\frac{1}{8}$ (SCORE 1 POINT; ½ IF YOU HAVE PUT 2.125).

Convert all the fractions into improper fractions:

1/5	2/5	3/5	4/5	5/5
1/3	3/3	5/3	7/3	9/3
1/4	4/4	7/4	10/4	13/4
1/8	5/8	9/8	13/8	($\frac{17}{8}$)

The final fraction could be: $\frac{17}{8}$ or $2\frac{1}{8}$

But as in the examples, improper fractions alternate with decimal fractions throughout. Also, as in the examples, the answer must be expressed in a unit and a fraction: $2\frac{1}{8}$

(You may have converted all the fractions into decimal fractions. In all but the second row this would have been valid, giving the final answer of 2.125. There are, however, two fallacies:

a) there are no perfect decimal fractions for $\frac{1}{3}$ or $1\frac{2}{3}$, as they are recurring decimals, as in 2.33 recurring;

b) the already established alternating sequence of improper and decimal fractions should be maintained.)

11 (C) (SCORE 1 POINT).

In the equations given, the number of straight strokes that form the letters is equal on each side. AZVN contains 11 straight strokes and KWE is the only one of the possible answers which also contains 11 straight strokes.

12 9 (SCORE 1 POINT).

The numbers move from one position clockwise at a time. Starting with 3 in the first square, the progression is:

3 4 5 6

Starting with 6 in the first square:

6 7 8 (9)

Starting with 5 in the first square:

5 6 7 8

Starting with 4 in the first square:

4 5 6 7

13 (SCORE 1 POINT IF ALL ARE CORRECT; ½ IF 8 OR 9.)

(A) CYGNET	(1) SIGNET
(B) ISLET	(2) EYELET
(C) ATE	(3) EIGHT
(D) NIGHT	(4) KNIGHT
(E) RING	(5) WRING
(F) PHARAOH	(6) FARO
(G) MALE	(7) MAIL
(H) CACHE	(8) CASH
(I) CEILING	(9) SEALING
(J) SELL	(10) CELL

14 55 (SCORE 1 POINT).

Divide the number on the left by 5 and multiply the number on the right by 5, entering the two results inside the brackets:

25 (55) 1

15 P (SCORE 1 POINT).

Give each letter a number according to its position in the alphabet. PEACE totals 30; HEA totals 14. Therefore, the 16th letter in the alphabet, which is P, must be added to bring the total up to 30.

Remember to keep a note of your score.

NOTES

4, 8 and 9 caused the most difficulty with the majority. The coincidence that there are 26 letters in the alphabet and 26 cards in half of a pack of cards is one that you may find used elsewhere in these tests, so it is worth bearing in mind. Substitution of numbers for letters according to the position of the letters in the alphabet may also be featured again and is worth remembering for the future.

TEST 3

Time limit: 30 minutes

1 If MEN equals 47147 and TEA equals 4471, which of the numbers below represents HIT?

(A) 471
(B) 1147
(C) 774
(D) 1441
(E) 447

2 Pair the emblems on the left with the places on the right.

(A) RED SUN	(1) CANADA
(B) LEEK	(2) GREAT BRITAIN
(C) SHAMROCK	(3) JAPAN
(D) MAPLE LEAF	(4) IRELAND
(E) STARS & STRIPES	(5) WALES
(F) UNION JACK	(6) UNITED STATES

3 Copy this grid and complete this crossword puzzle from the words listed on the left.

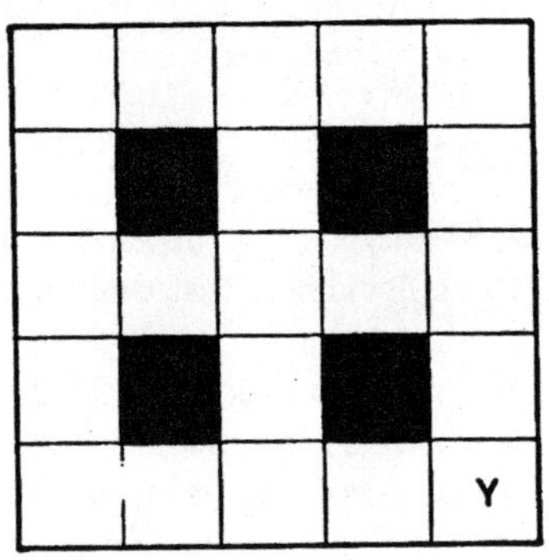

ANGER
ASTER
BATON
BLUSH
CARRY
CHASM
CIGAR
COMIC
CRASH
CUBIC
HONEY
HURRY
MONEY
ORGAN

4 Which of the figures at the bottom should follow 3 at the top?

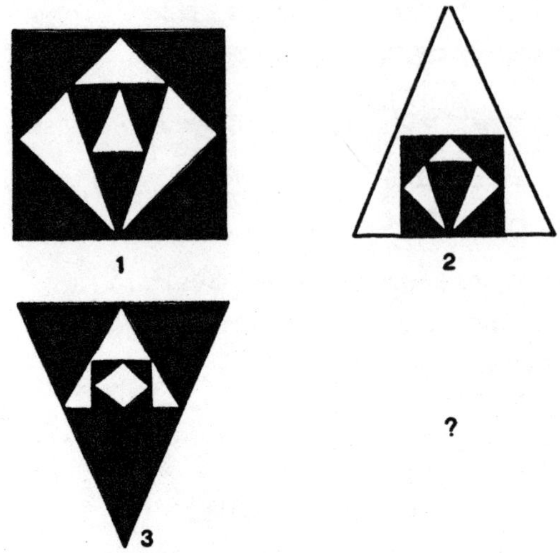

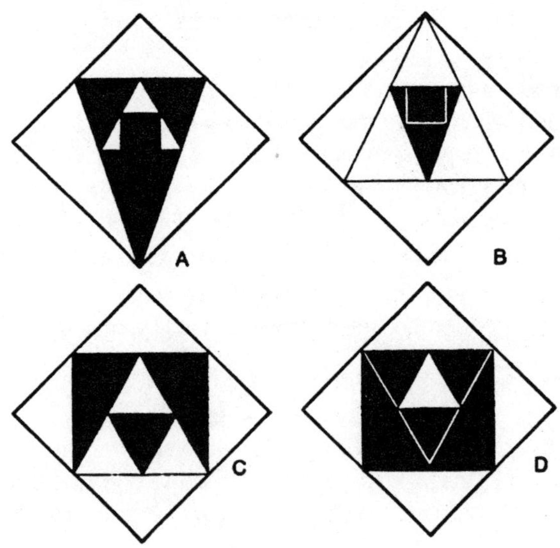

5 What are x and y?

A	A	B	B	12
A	B	C	B	19
B	x	A	B	17
y	C	A	A	18
13	22	17	14	

6 Which book is wrong?

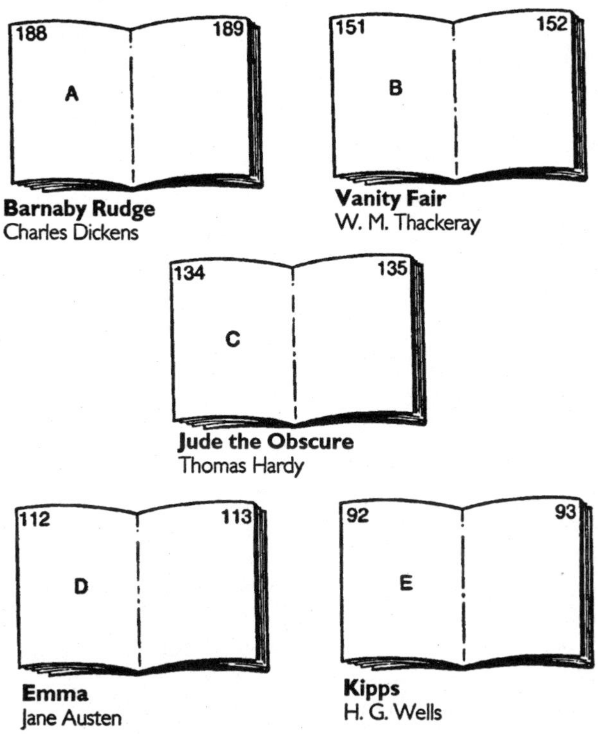

7 Which number from 1 to 9 is x?

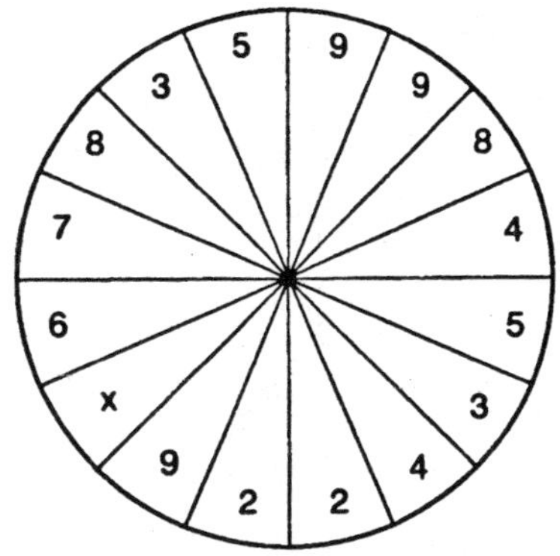

8 Which is the odd one out?

(A) I AM LAW
(B) SWAN BOAT
(C) I AM A NIB
(D) LOST HOE
(E) NEAR GIANT

9 What is x?

1	2	3	2	10	12
2	5	12	10	16	13
1	2	1	x	10	24

10 Multiply the square root of the highest number by the square of the lowest number.

144	6	169	7	152
5	166	9	158	8
3	168	4	167	10

11 A closet has been removed from a room, leaving a space on the floor with no carpet. The rest of the floor is carpeted, and fortunately there are some pieces of carpet left over. Which two pieces will fit the empty space and exactly match the existing carpet?

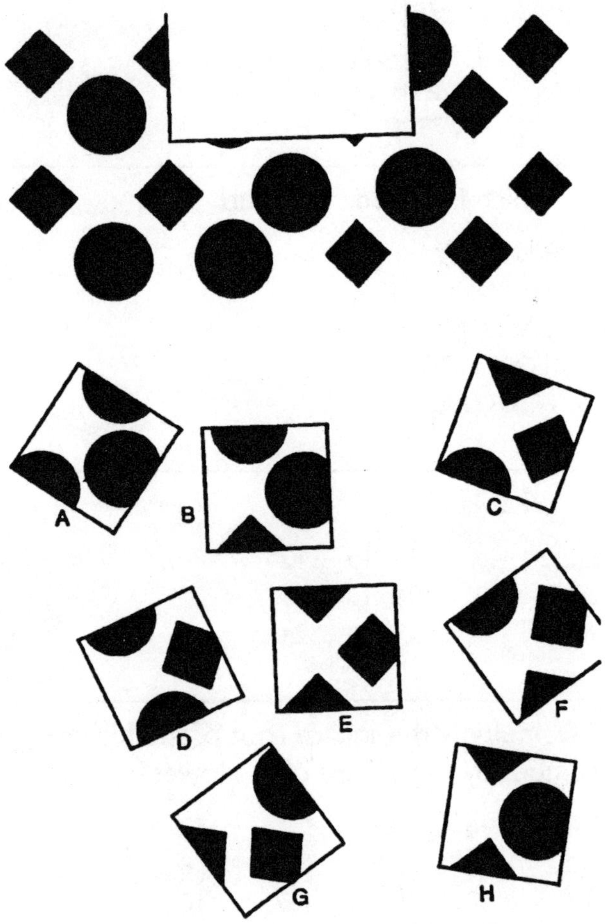

12 What is x?

4 9 1 3 2 2 3 5 5 7 9 x

13 Pair the given name in the first column with the surnames in the second column.

(A) CHARLES	(1) MILTON
(B) WILLIAM	(2) MARLOWE
(C) JAMES	(3) LEACOCK
(D) HILAIRE	(4) KINGSLEY
(E) JOHN	(5) CHAUCER
(F) CHRISTOPHER	(6) BLAKE
(G) EDWARD	(7) SPENSER
(H) EDMUND	(8) BELLOC
(I) STEPHEN	(9) BARRIE
(J) GEOFFREY	(10) LEAR

14 Which word is spelled wrong?

(A) EMBARRASS
(B) SIEGE
(C) ACCOMMODATE
(D) HARASS
(E) DECEIVE
(F) PUSILANIMOUS
(G) CATALYST

15 Here is part of a jigsaw puzzle on which a triangle is marked. Which is the missing piece?

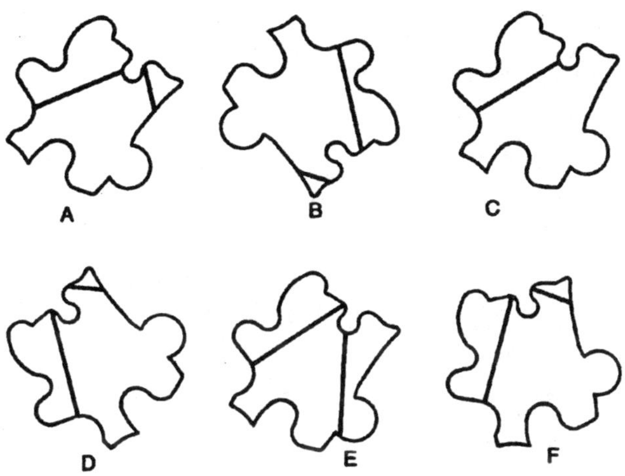

ANSWERS TO TEST 3

1 (A) **(SCORE 1 POINT).**

(This problem was deliberately positioned near question 11 in the previous test to see whether you have benefited from reading the explanations.)

The number of straight lines that make up the words agrees with the number of straight lines that make up the numbers. 471 is the only figure that has the same number of strokes, six, as HIT.

2 (A) (3); (B) (5); (C) (4); (D) (1); (E) (6); (F) (2) **(SCORE 1 POINT IF ALL ARE CORRECT).**

3 **(SCORE 1 POINT FOR EITHER OF THE FOLLOWING.)**

C	U	B	I	C
H		A		A
A	S	T	E	R
S		O		R
M	O	N	E	Y

C	H	A	S	M
U		S		O
B	A	T	O	N
I		E		E
C	A	R	R	Y

4 A **(SCORE 1 POINT).**

The smallest figure in the center becomes the largest figure on the outside, while the other figures remain in the same order.

5 x is 7; y is 5 **(SCORE 1 POINT IF BOTH ARE CORRECT).**

Incidentally, A is 2, B is 4 and C is 9.39

6 B **(SCORE 1 POINT).**

Even page numbers always appear on the verso (left) and odd numbers always appear on the recto (right).

7 2 **(SCORE 1 POINT).**

Starting at 7 and working clockwise, two adjacent numbers in the top semicircle are added. In the opposite segments are factors of that total:

$7 + 8 = 15;$ $3 \times 5 = 15$
$3 + 5 = 8;$ $2 \times 4 = 8$
$9 + 9 = 18;$ $9 \times 2 = 18$

Hence:

$8 + 4 = 12;$ $6 \times 2 = 12$

8 (E) **(SCORE 1 POINT).**

This is an anagram of ARGENTINA, which is in South America. All the others are in Africa:

(A) MALAWI
(B) BOTSWANA
(C) NAMIBIA
(D) LESOTHO

9 13 **(SCORE 1 POINT).**

The totals of the columns are:

4 9 16 ? 36 49

In other words, 2 squared, 3 squared, 4 squared, etc.

10 117 **(SCORE 1 POINT).**

11 B and D **(SCORE 1 POINT IF BOTH ARE CORRECT; ½ IF ONE).**

12 2 **(SCORE 1 POINT).**

Spaced correctly the series becomes:

4 9 13 22 35 57 9(2)

After the first two numbers, each subsequent number is the total of the previous two. The sum of 35 and 57 is 92.

13 (A) (4); (B) (6); (C) (9); (D) (8); (E) (1); (F) (2); (G) (10); (H) (7); (I) (3); (J) (5) **(SCORE 1 POINT IF ALL ARE CORRECT; ½ IF 8 OR 9).**

14 (F) **(SCORE 1 POINT).**

It should be spelled PUSILLANIMOUS (meaning cowardly).

15 B **(SCORE 1 POINT).**

REMEMBER TO KEEP A NOTE OF YOUR SCORE ON PAGE 45.

NOTES

3, 5, 7, and 11 gave the greatest difficulty, and 3 should have taken the most time. 6 was easy unless you were preoccupied with the authors and titles, searching for a discrepancy in one or the other. 11 was tricky and definitely trying on the eyes! The patterns were so similar and it was not easy to differentiate between the left and the right halves of the bare space.

TEST 4

Time limit: 25 minutes

1 What number goes into the empty brackets?

916 (160) 916
971 (177) 879
245 ( ) 511

2 Which is the odd one out?

(A) $15/16$
(B) $11/13$
(C) $2/3$
(D) $4/7$
(E) $5/17$

3 Go from DOVER to PARIS in six moves, changing one letter at a time.

DOVER
1 – – – – –
2 – – – – –
3 – – – – –
4 – – – – –
5 – – – – –
6 PARIS

4 What comes between 16 and 4 in this series?

6561 256 81 16 – 4 3

5 Which is the odd one out?

(A) AFGHAN
(B) STUPOR
(C) INDIAN
(D) DEFIANT
(E) LAUGHING

6 Without using a straight edge, if AB and XY are joined, which number will be nearest to the point of intersection?

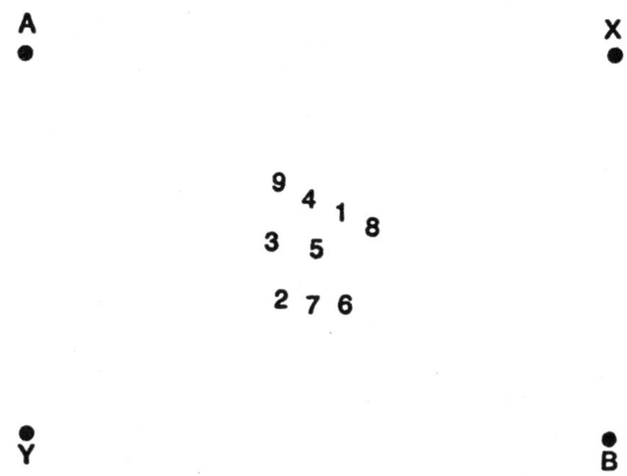

7 Complete this series:

1 2 3 5 8 13 21 34 55 –

8 Which is the odd one out?

(A) STOP
(B) YARD
(C) PANS
(D) EMIR
(E) KNAR
(F) NIPS
(G) TRAY

9 A train leaves Womensville for Manstown with twice as many women passengers as men. At Middleton 16 women get off and 17 men get on. There are now the same number of each. How many passengers left Womensville?

10 What letter takes the place of x?

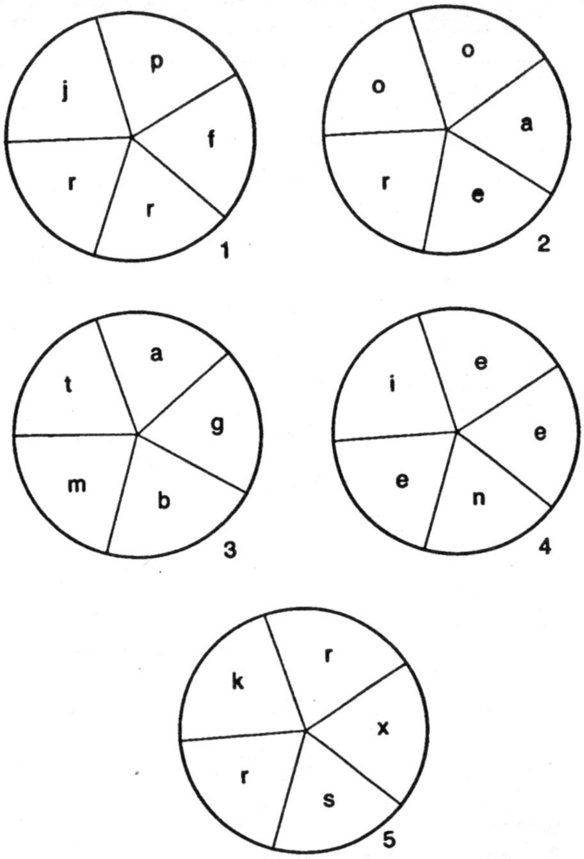

11 Which is the odd one out?

(A) TEAL
(B) COB
(C) PEN
(D) CYGNET
(E) SWAN

12

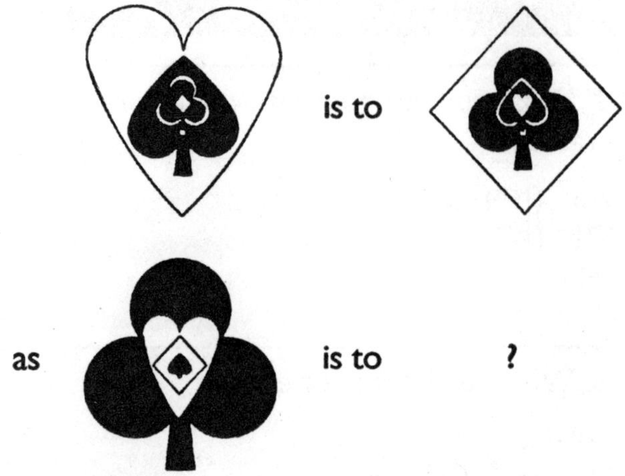

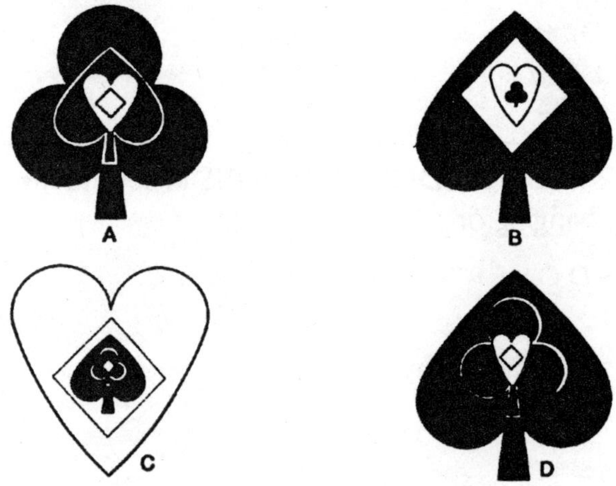

13 Six of these keys will open the door. Which one won't?

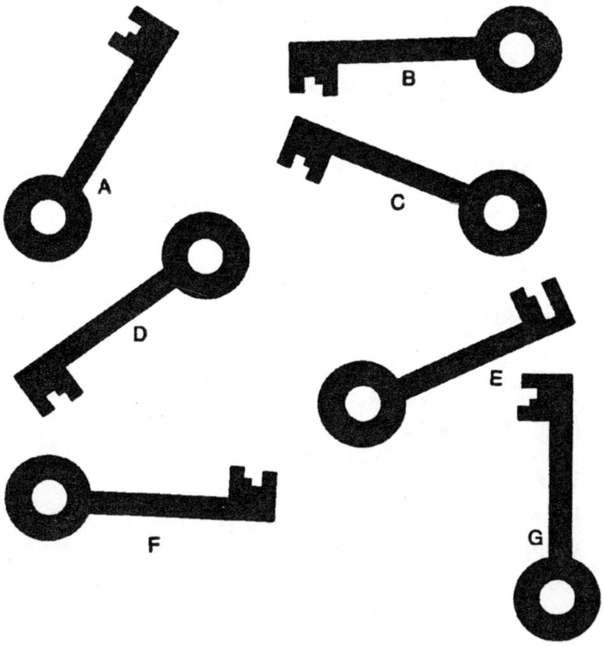

14 Pair these words to make nine titles of books by Charles Dickens:

(A) LITTLE	(1) RUDGE
(B) PICKWICK	(2) COPPERFIELD
(C) EDWIN	(3) TIMES
(D) BARNABY	(4) CHUZZLEWIT
(E) NICHOLAS	(5) PAPERS
(F) HARD	(6) HOUSE
(G) BLEAK	(7) DROOD
(H) DAVID	(8) DORRIT
(I) MARTIN	(9) NICKLEBY

15 Which screw is different?

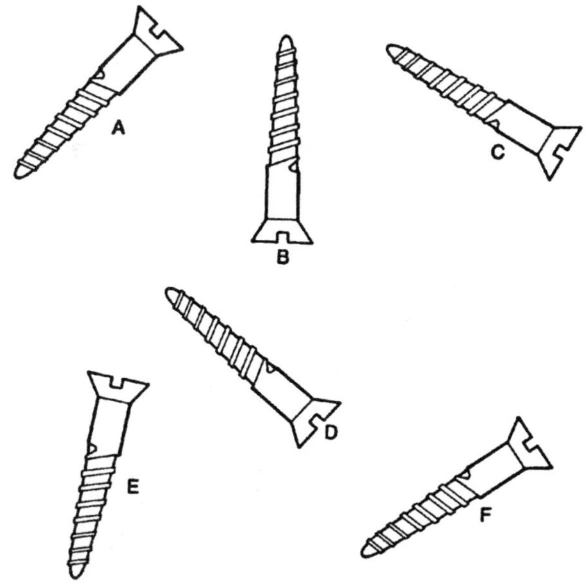

NOW CHECK YOUR ANSWERS AND KEEP A NOTE OF YOUR SCORE ON PAGE 45.

ANSWERS TO TEST 4

1 114 **(SCORE 1 POINT).**

The two numbers on the left inside the brackets are the sum of the digits on the left of the brackets. The number on the right inside the brackets is the difference between the sums of the digits on either side of the brackets.

2 A **(SCORE 1 POINT).**

It is the only fraction which contains an odd number (15) which is NOT a prime number. All the other fractions contain even numbers or odd numbers which are primary numbers.

3 **(SCORE 1 POINT. IF YOU HAVE USED OTHER WORDS YOU MAY SCORE 1 POINT, PROVIDED THEY ARE GENUINE.)**

DOVER
1 DOVES
2 ROVES
3 RAVES
4 PAVES
5 PARES
6 PARIS

4 9 **(SCORE 1 POINT)**

There are two separate series here. Starting with the first term and taking alternate terms thereafter:

6561 81 9 3

Each number is the square root of the previous number.

Starting with the second term:

256 16 4

Again, each number is the square root of the previous number.

5 (C) **(SCORE 1 POINT).**

All the other words contain three consecutive letters of the alphabet.

(A) a F G H a n
(B) S T U p o r
(D) D E F i a n t
(E) l a u G H I n g

6 5 **(SCORE 1 POINT).**

This is at the EXACT point of intersection.

7 89 **(SCORE 1 POINT).**

Starting with 3, each number is the sum of the two previous numbers. Thus the final term is the sum of 34 and 55.

8 (G) **(SCORE 1 POINT).**

All the other words make words when reversed:

(A) STOP – POTS
(B) YARD – DRAY
(C) PANS – SNAP
(D) EMIR – RIME
(E) KNAR – RANK
(F) NIPS – SPIN

9 99 **(SCORE 1 POINT).**

Let x represent the number of men who get on at Womensville. The number of passengers who start the journey is 3x.

At Middleton:

$2x-16=x+7$,

therefore:

$x=33$

We already know that twice as many women started the journey, so there must have been 66 women and 33 men.

10 n **(SCORE 1 POINT).**

Starting with j in the first circle and considering every second segment thereafter in the succeeding circles, you get:

james

Starting with p in the first circle and proceeding in the same way:

peter

Starting with f in the first circle and proceeding in the same way:

frank

Starting with the first r in the first circle and proceeding in the same way:

roger

Starting with the second r in the first circle and proceeding in the same way:

robi(n)

11 (A) **(SCORE 1 POINT).**

A teal is a duck. All the others are swans.

12 B **(SCORE 1 POINT).**

The very small center suit becomes the large outer suit. The next smallest inner suit becomes the next largest outer suit. The next smallest inner suit becomes the next largest outer suit. The largest outer suit becomes the smallest center suit.

13 E **(SCORE 1 POINT).**

The teeth (the projections at the end) which turn the lock are different from those in the other keys.

14 (A) (8); (B) (5); (C) (7); (D) (1); (E) (9); (F) (3); (G) (6); (H) (2); (I) (4) **(SCORE 1 POINT IF ALL ARE CORRECT; ½ IF 7 OR 8).**

15 C **(SCORE 1 POINT).**

The thread turns the opposite way from the others.

Keep a note of your score.

NOTES

1, 4, 9 and 10 presented the most problems. If you solved 9 by algebra, as given in the explanation, it would have not have held you up for long. If you relied on trial and error it would probably have taken longer. In 10, which stumped many, the letters were deliberately printed in lower case so as to throw you off the track that they were proper names.

RATINGS AND IQ SCORES FOR GROUP II

TEST 1	Average 5½ points
TEST 2	Average 6 points
TEST 3	Average 8 points
TEST 4	Average 9 points

TOTAL FOR THE GROUP

(Out of a possible 60 points)

Over 48	Excellent
43-48	Very Good
29-42	Good
28½	Average
22-28	Fair
Under 22	Poor

YOUR SCORES FOR CHALLENGING TESTS

TEST 1	______
TEST 2	______
TEST 3	______
TEST 4	______
TOTAL	______

SEE IQ SCORING INSTRUCTIONS ON PAGE 63

GROUP III

MASTERFUL

TEST 1

Time limit: 1 hour (After 30 minutes take a break and then resume for the next 30 minutes)

1 Here is a sign of the zodiac in code:

From this you must now break this naval message received in code:

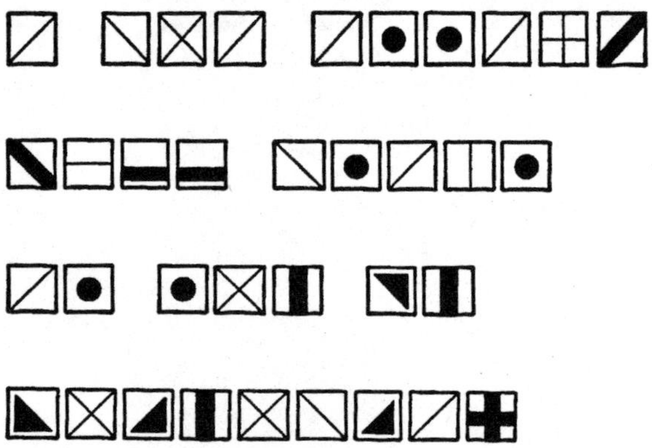

2 What is x?

A 2 D 7 x 16 V 29

3 What comes next in this series?

8 E 2 T 6 S 9
N 3 T 4 F 5 -

4 The ball in A moves clockwise, first one place, then two places, then three, and so on. When it lands on an even number the ball in B moves clockwise; when it lands on an odd number the ball in B moves counter-clockwise. The ball in B also moves first one place, then two places, then three, and so on. After six moves what number will the ball in B finish on?

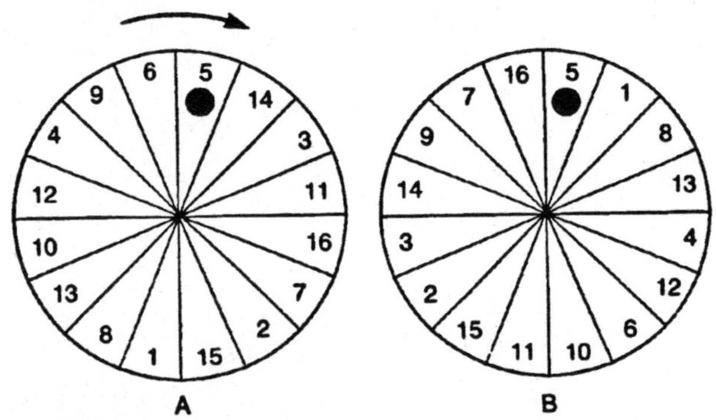

5 What are x and y in this series?

1 4 3 12 6 30 10 50 15 60 x y

6 Which is the odd one out?

(A) GREGORY
(B) NORMAN
(C) WILLIAM

7 Which is the odd one out?

(A) TRINITY
(B) ALLEGHENY
(C) ERIE
(D) DELAWARE
(E) PEARL
(F) WABASH
(G) CHEYENNE

8 Assuming that you have no disabilities, where can you place your left hand where your right hand cannot touch it?

9 Arrange these into four pairs:

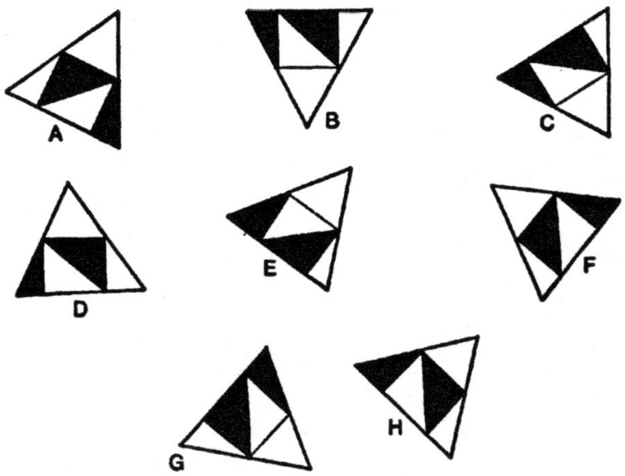

10 What should take the place of x?

2 4 5 3 4 6 7 5 6 8 9 x

11 What are x, y and z?

76 69 52 65 60 45 54 51 38
43 42 31 32 33 24 x y z

12 Form ten related pairs from these words:

GOAL TELEVISION CAR SUN STROKE
MAJOR HIGH BREAST SET KEEPER MASTER
GARAGE PICKET DRUM SERGEANT FENCE
COLOR HEAD RISE PIECE

13 Which is the greatest

(A) 1/4 of 236
(B) 1/16 of 1028
(C) 1/9 of 504
(D) 1/13 of 741
(E) 1/17 of 1020

14 Which of the numbers in the bottom line should take the place of x?

121 252 x 182 255
63 128 104 255 301 336

15 What is x?

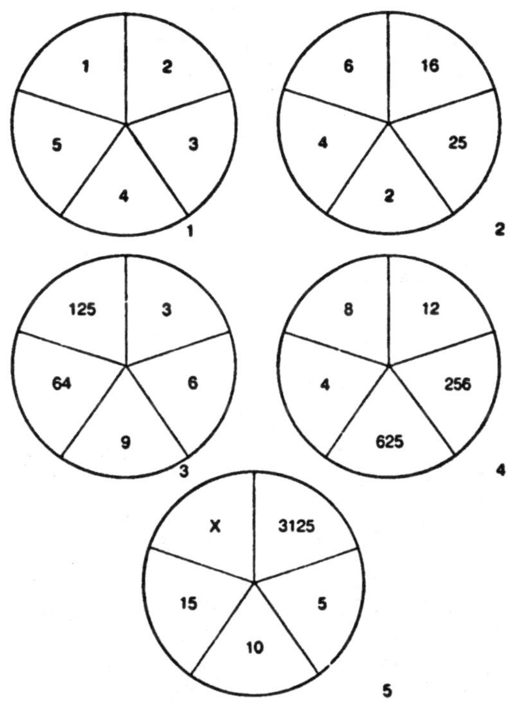

NOW CHECK YOUR ANSWERS AND KEEP A NOTE OF YOUR SCORE ON PAGE 62.

1 A SEA ATTACK WILL START AT TEN ON WEDNESDAY (SCORE 1 POINT).

The only signs of the zodiac which contain five letters are ARIES, LIBRA and VIRGO. In the coded message the first word has only one letter, corresponding with the first letter in the zodiac sign. As this cannot be L or V, it follows that the zodiac sign is ARIES. This supplies five symbols which can now be substituted in the message:

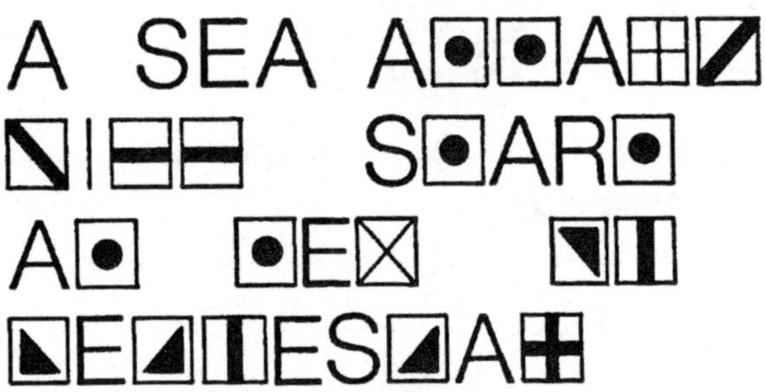

The two-letter word that starts line three begins with A, and the only possibilities are M, N or T (S has already been accounted for). Whatever this letter is, it is repeated twice in both the second word and the fifth word. In the latter case, there are no such words as SMARM or SNARN, so that only leaves T. (Also, T is probably the most commonly used consonant, and is featured no fewer than six times in the message.)

So the fifth word is START and the sixth word is AT. Also, the third word, as we now know, starts with ATTA — and (remember we are dealing with a naval message) ATTACK is a reasonable assumption. In fact, the only six-letter words which start this way are ATTACH, ATTACK and ATTAIN. It cannot be ATTAIN, because I has already been accounted for. The fourth word ends with a double letter: –I––. This double letter cannot be A, B, C, D, G, H, J, K, M, N, O, P, Q, R, T, U, V, W, X, Y or Z, and must be F or L. As the only words ending in FF are BIFF, JIFF and TIFF — none of which is likely and the T is already accounted for—it is more probable that it ends in LL: –ILL. It is clearly BILL, DILL, FILL, GILL, HILL, KILL, MILL, PILL or WILL, and the most likely choices are KILL or WILL. If it is KILL, it means that the last word starts with KE, but with the letters already fitted, (and using reasonable deduction) the choice is almost bound to be WE, and the full word itself, WEDNESDAY, should fall into place from WE-N (N has already been deduced from the seventh word: TE-) ES-A-(W was deduced from WILL earlier). From the context of what has now been solved it should be clear which symbols represent O (as in the eighth word) and D and Y (as in the last word).

You may have decoded this message using different methods, but the important thing is to arrive at the correct solution, whether through inspired guessing or clever deduction.

2 11 (SCORE 1 POINT).

Substituting numbers for letters, according to the position in the alphabet of the letters, the series becomes:

1 2 4 7 x 16 22 29

The numbers are increasing by 1, 2, 3, etc. So x will be 7 + 4.

3 F (SCORE 1 POINT).

Each letter is the initial letter of the letter preceding it: 8 (Eight), 2 (Two), etc., and so 5 (Five).

4 9 (SCORE 1 POINT).

The moves are as follows:

	A	B
1st move	14	1
2nd move	11	16
3rd move	2	8
4th move	13	7
5th move	6	13
6th move	7	9

5 x is 21; y is 84 (SCORE 1 POINT IF BOTH ARE CORRECT; ½ IF ONE).

There are two series here. Starting with the first term and proceeding alternately:

1 3 6 10 15

The terms increase by 2, 3, 4 and 5. Therefore 15 must be increased by 6, making x 21.

In the second series, preceding ODD numbers are multiplied by 4 and preceding EVEN numbers are multiplied by 5, which gives:

4	(1x4)
12	(3x4)
30	(6x5)
50	(10x5)
60	(15x4)

So y is 21x4.

6 (C) **(SCORE 1 POINT).**

Although they are all boys' names, (A) and (B) also contain other boys' names in reverse: ROGER and RON.

7 (C) **(SCORE 1 POINT).**

Except for (C), these are all names of major North American Rivers. (C) Erie is a Great Lake.

8 On your right elbow **(SCORE 1 POINT).**

This is the only place which is completely out of reach of the right hand.

9 AF; BC; DH; EG **(SCORE 1 POINT IF ALL ARE CORRECT).**

10 7 **(SCORE 1 POINT).**

Each pair of digits is reversed and has 1 added to each digit to become the next pair. Thus 24, reversed and with 1 added to 2 and 1 added to 4, becomes 53, 53 becomes 46, 46 becomes 75, 75 becomes 68. Therefore 68 must become 97.

11 x is 21; y is 24; z is 17 **(SCORE 1 POINT IF ALL ARE CORRECT; ½ IF 2).**

There are three separate series here. Starting with the first term and taking every third term thereafter:

76 65 54 43 32

As they reduce by 11 each time, the next term, x, must be 21.

From the second term and proceeding in the same way, we get:

69 60 51 42 33

These reduce by 9 each time, so the next term, y, is 24.

From the third term, we get:

52 45 38 31 24

As these reduce by 7 each time, the next term, z, is 17.

12 **(SCORE 1 POINT IF ALL ARE CORRECT; ½ IF 8 OR 9.)**

GOAL KEEPER; PICKET FENCE; CAR GARAGE; SUN SET; HIGH RISE; COLOR TELEVISION; SERGEANT MAJOR; DRUM HEAD; MASTER PIECE; BREAST STROKE

13 (B) **(SCORE 1 POINT).**

(A) 59
(B) 64¼
(C) 56
(D) 57
(E) 60

14 104 **(SCORE 1 POINT).**

121 is divisible by 11;
252 is divisible by 12;
104 (x) is divisible by 13;
182 is divisible by 14;
255 is divisible by 15.

15 1024 **(SCORE 1 POINT).**

Start at 1 in the first circle and move clockwise throughout, missing two segments each time:

1 2 3 4 5

The numbers increase by 1 each time.
Starting at 2 in the first circle:

2 4 6 8 10

The numbers increase by 2 each time.
Starting at 3 in the first circle:

3 6 9 12 15

The numbers increase by three each time.
Starting at 4 in the first circle:

4 16 64 256 1024 (x)

The numbers were multiplied by 4 each time.
Starting at 5 in the first circle:

5 25 125 625 3125

The numbers were multiplied by 5 each time.

Remember to keep a note of your score.

NOTES

4, 5, 11 and 15 caused the greatest difficulty and took the longest time. Surprisingly, 1 did not present the difficulty nor wasted the time expected. It was either solved comparatively quickly or not solved at all. Once it was realized that the zodiac sign had to be ARIES, the rest seemed to fall into place without much complication.

Again, 3 was either surprisingly difficult or surprisingly easy. If it was realized quickly that the letters were the initials of the numbers, the answer came almost immediately; if not, there was simply nothing to go on, as there was no noticeable regularity of any kind in the series.

The time limit was generous enough to allow for the amount of working-out involved with 1, 4 and 12.

TEST 2

Time limit: 1 hour 15 minutes
(take a break after 45 minutes and then resume for the next 30 minutes)

1 Give values for A, B, C, and D.

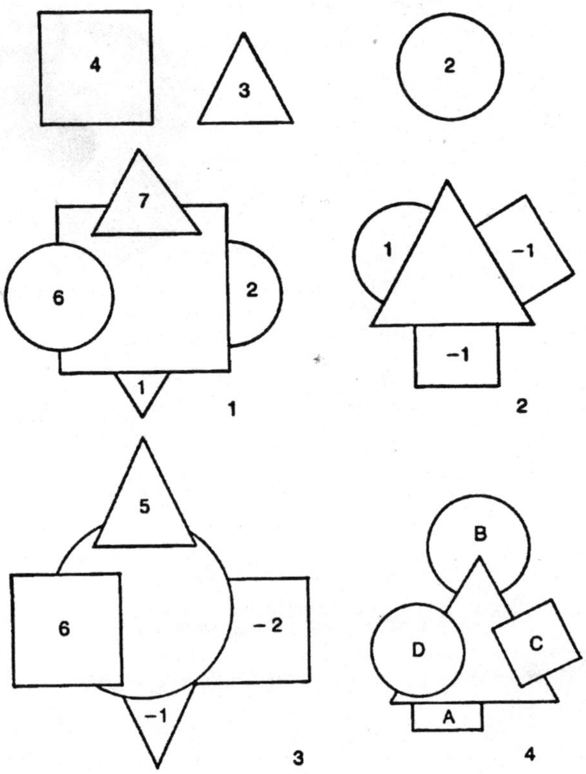

2 The two cards at the top should enable you to solve the word underneath.

3 Which one follows No. 6?

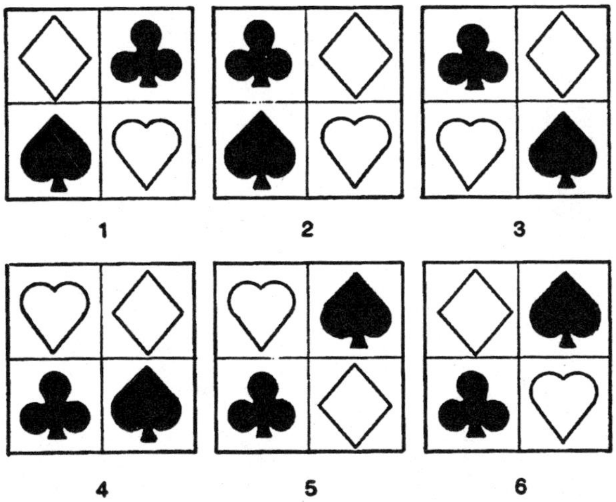

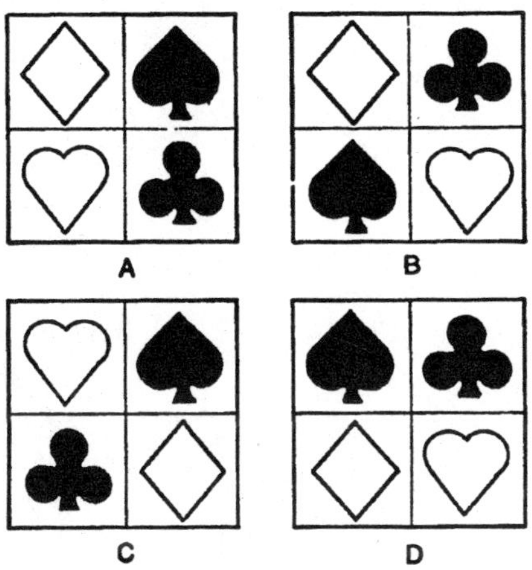

4 Which triangle is wrong?

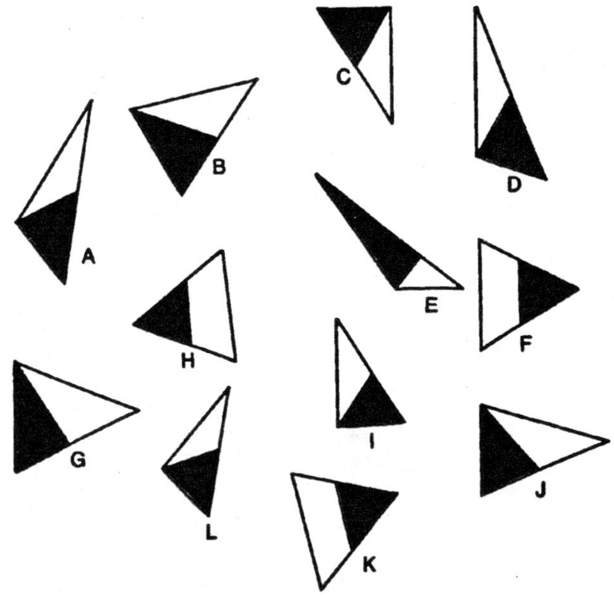

5 Pair words in the first column with words in the second column, finishing with ten connected or related pairs:

(A) OVER	(1) TEAM
(B) RUST	(2) ROOM
(C) DRAWING	(3) BELT
(D) NON	(4) LAST
(E) OUT	(5) PIN
(F) HOME	(6) SENSE
(G) SHELL	(7) STEAD
(H) HAIR	(8) FISH
(I) HEAD	(9) CAST
(J) IN	(10) BOARD

6 Subtract the sum of the prime numbers from the sum of the odd numbers (which are not prime) and add the sum of the even numbers:

3	6	7	9
11	12	14	15
16	18	19	21
27	31	33	

7

If

is FOG

and

is GEM

and

is HIM

what is this?

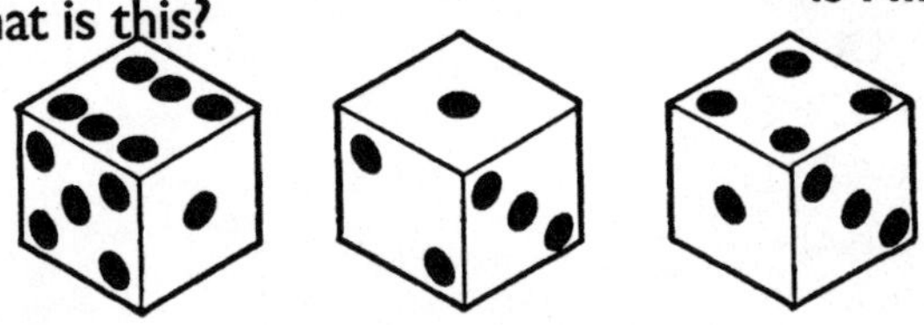

8 Three of these days have one thing in common. Which day does not share this common feature?

(A) MONDAY
(B) TUESDAY
(C) THURSDAY
(D) SATURDAY

9 Which is the odd one out?

(A) 119
(B) 21
(C) 91
(D) 77
(E) 95
(F) 105

10

If

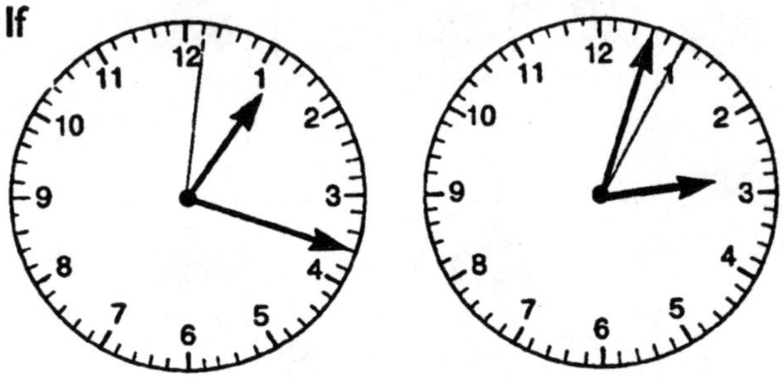

is France,

what is this?

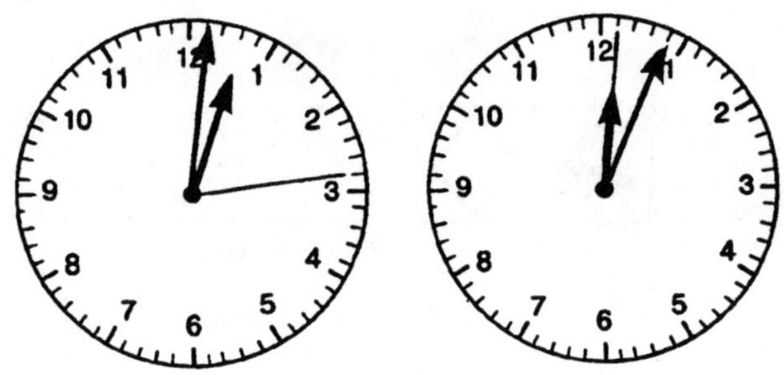

11 If GILBERT is -1, NORMAN is 37, FRED is 23 and ARTHUR is 4, what is EDWARD?

12 What are the next two terms in this series?

36 91 21 51 82 12 42 7 –

13 What are A, B and C?

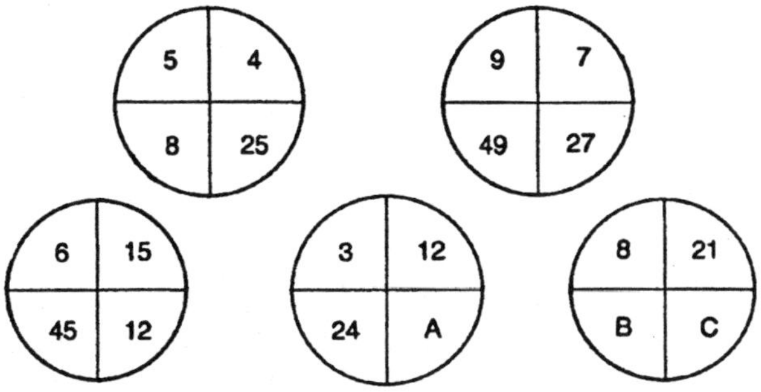

14 Which of the fractions in the bottom line should complete the series in the top line?

3.8 $\frac{29}{6}$ $5\frac{6}{7}$ 6.875

$7\frac{1}{4}$ 8.1 $\frac{77}{9}$ $\frac{71}{9}$ 8.375

15 If $\frac{PIG}{8}$ is D and $\frac{DOG}{13}$ is B,

what is this?

$\frac{CAT}{4}$

NOW CHECK YOUR ANSWERS AND KEEP A NOTE OF YOUR SCORE ON PAGE 62.

ANSWERS TO TEST 2

1 A is -1; B is 1; C is 7; D is 5 **(SCORE 1 POINT IF ALL ARE CORRECT; ½ IF 3).**

We know that a square is worth 4 points, a triangle 3 points and a circle 2 points.

A figure lying ABOVE another adds its value to that of the one below. A figure lying BENEATH another deducts its value from the one above. So, in the first diagram:

The top triangle (3) adds its value to the square beneath it (4) and is worth 7; the circle on the left (2) adds its value to the square beneath it (4) and is worth 6; the bottom triangle subtracts its value (3) from that of the square (4) and is worth 1; the circle on the right subtracts its value (2) from that of the square (4) and is worth 2.

Thus in the last diagram:

square A is worth -1 (3 - 4);

circle B is worth 1 (3 - 2)

square C is worth 7 (4 + 3)

circle D is worth 5 (3 + 2)

2 APTITUDE **(SCORE 1 POINT).**

Another problem based on the 26 letters of the alphabet corresponding with the 26 cards in two suits. Here hearts represent A to M (ace to king); diamonds represent N to Z (ace to king).

Ace of hearts	1st letter	A
3 of diamonds	16th letter	P
7 of diamonds	20th letter	T
9 of hearts	9th letter	I
7 of diamonds	20th letter	T
8 of diamonds	21st letter	U
4 of hearts	4th letter	D
5 of hearts	5th letter	E

3 B **(SCORE 1 POINT).**

In square 2 the top two suits in square 1 are transposed. In square 3 the bottom two suits in square 2 are transposed. In square 4 the left vertical column in square 3 is transposed. In square 5 the right vertical column in square 4 is transposed. In square 6 the top left has been transposed with the bottom right in square 5. Therefore, in the next square the top right will be transposed with the bottom left in square 6.

4 E **(SCORE 1 POINT).**

There are four different types of triangle here:

equilateral (all sides equal)

isosceles (two sides equal)

right-angled (one right angle)

scalene (all sides unequal)

Each is shaded according to its type, the scalene triangle being shaded like this:

In E, however, it is shaded like this:

5 (A) (9); (B) (3); (C) (10); (D) (6); (E) (4); (F) (1); (G) (8); (H) (5); (I) (2); (J) (7) **(SCORE 1 POINT IF ALL ARE CORRECT; ½ IF 8 OR 9). You may score 1 point if you have used other combinations of words—but only if you have all ten correct.**

6 100 **(SCORE 1 POINT).**

7 ICE **(SCORE 1 POINT).**

In the first row the spots on each cube are added and given letters equal to their position in the alphabet:

6 (F) 15 (O) 7 (G)

In the second row 1 is deducted from the total of the spots on each cube. In the third row 2 is deducted from each total. In the last row 3 is deducted from each total:

12-3=9 (I)

6-3=3 (C)

8-3=5 (E)

8 (A) **(SCORE 1 POINT).**

The others contain two consecutive letters of the alphabet:

(B) TUesday

(C) thuRSday

(D) saTUrday

9 (E) **(SCORE 1 POINT).**

All the other numbers are divisible by 7.

10 CANADA **(SCORE 1 POINT).**

The hour hand of the first clock is at 6; the sixth letter of the alphabet is F. The minute hand is at 18: R. The second hand is at 1: A. On the second clock, the hour hand is at 14: N. The minute hand is at 3: C. The second hand is at 5: E. Follow the same principle for the other to clocks and you get CANADA.

11 -27 **(SCORE 1 POINT).**

Substitute numbers for letters according to their alphabetical position. Add the value of the first and second letters, subtract the third, add the next, then subtract, and so on:

E(5)+D(4)-W(23)+A(1)-R(18)+D(4)

5+4-23+1-18+4=-27

12 3 and 0 **(SCORE 1 POINT IF BOTH ARE CORRECT).**

The series must be spaced correctly:

3 6 9 12 15 18 21 24 27

The terms increase by 3 throughout, so 30 is next.

13 A is 9; B is 63; C is 16 **(SCORE 1 POINT IF ALL ARE CORRECT).**

Prime numbers are squared in the opposite quarter; even numbers are doubled in the opposite quarter; odd numbers are tripled in the opposite quarter.

14 $\frac{71}{9}$ **(SCORE 1 POINT).**

Convert all the fractions in the top line into improper fractions:

$3\frac{4}{5}$ $4\frac{5}{6}$ $5\frac{6}{7}$ $6\frac{7}{8}$

This establishes the pattern:

345 456 567 678

So the final fraction must represent 789, which is $\frac{71}{9}$.

15 F **(SCORE 1 POINT).**

If each letter has a value according to its position in the alphabet, the total of each word is as follows:

P I G . . . 32

D O G . . . 26

C A T . . . 24

32(PIG)÷8=4 — that is, D (the 4th letter)

26(DOG)÷13=2—that is, B (the 2nd letter)

24 (CAT)÷4=6—that is, F (the 6th letter)

Remember to keep a note of your score.

NOTES

If you have followed these tests and explanations through, 2 should not have given too much trouble, as it is based on a question-type used before. 5, 7, 10 and 11 were the most time-consuming.

The incorrectly spaced series in 12 (the answer becomes very obvious when it is correctly spaced) should also have not been too troublesome to ardent followers of these tests. Previously I have advised you to keep a look-out for series which are incorrectly spaced.

In 8 the strange coincidence of two consecutive letters in alphabetical order eluded many—probably because it was so obvious!

11 was very difficult, but the clue lay in the minus value given for GILBERT, which should have indicated that there had to be deductions as well as additions.

TEST 3

Time limit: 35 minutes

1 Which of the figures below should occupy the vacant space?

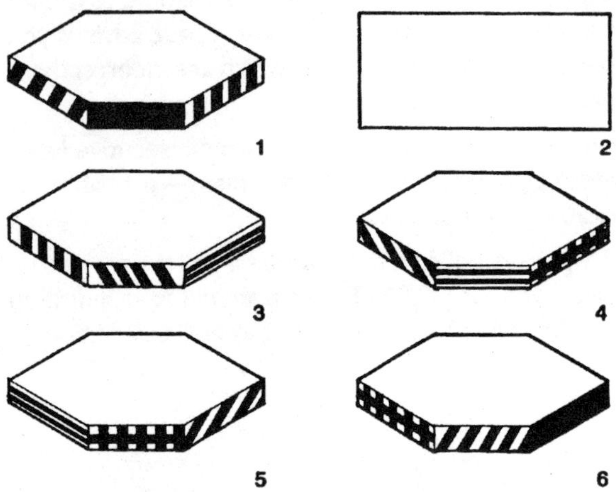

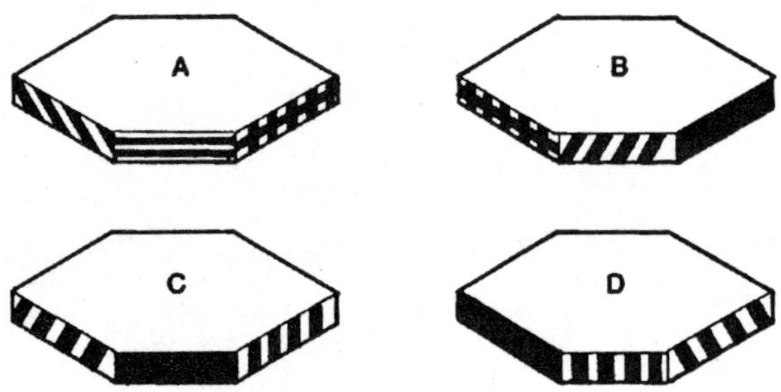

2 Which is the odd one out?

(A) BUCOLIC
(B) DIATRIBE
(C) LATIN
(D) HOURI
(E) JACK
(F) LOCUM

3 Here is a roulette wheel. When the ball stops at zero all the stakes go to the casino. The ball travels counterclockwise. At the first spin it stops at the next number. Then it misses one and stops at the next. After that each spin brings the ball one extra number along (missing two, then three, and so on). At what spin will the stakes go to the casino?

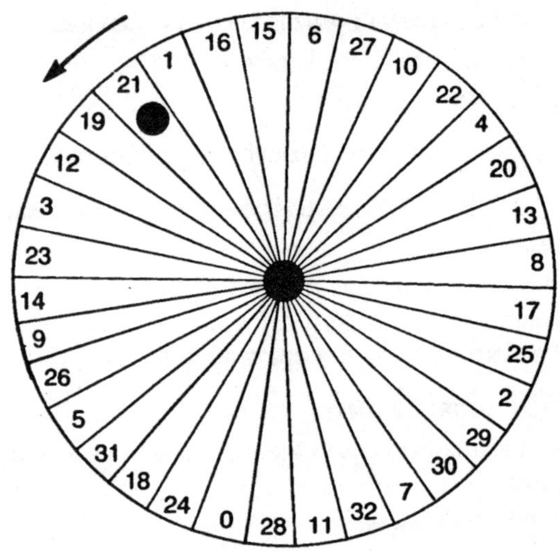

4 If CHOP is LARK, what letter completes the second word here?

FREE is DAR-

5 The top four cards should enable you to find the word represented by the bottom six cards.

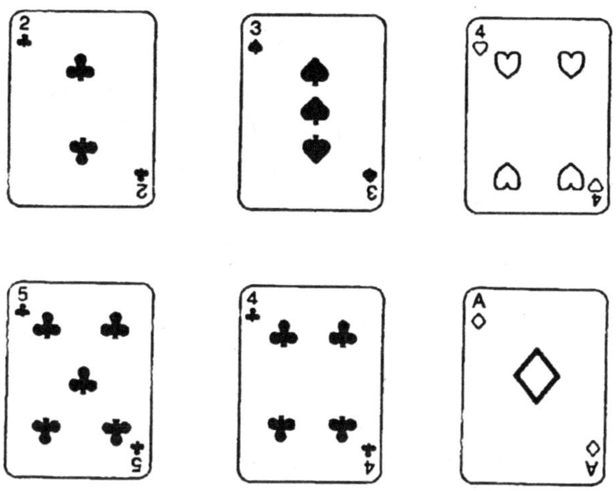

6 Which is the odd one out?

(A) BEGIN
(B) AIR
(C) DEFT
(D) WOLF
(E) BELOW
(F) BEG
(G) NOW

7 Arrange these into four pairs.

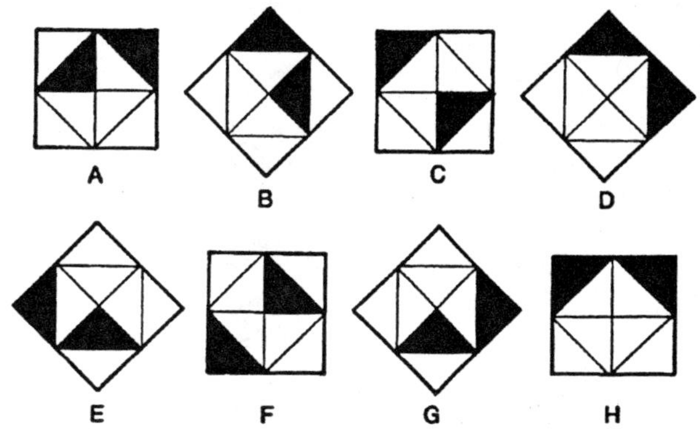

8 What goes into the empty space?

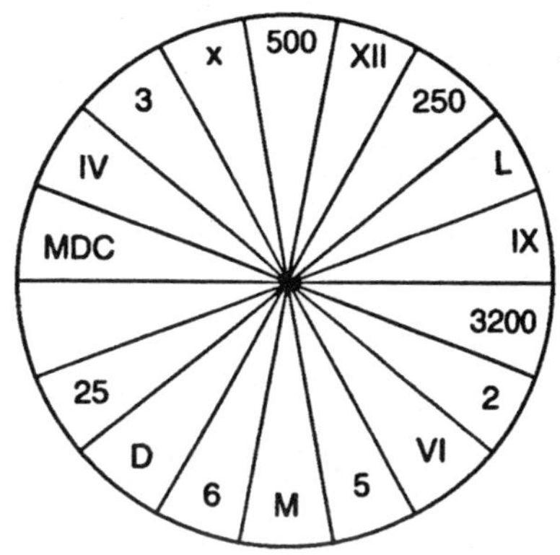

9 What comes next?

GELN-

10 Which of the cubes at the bottom should follow the two at the top?

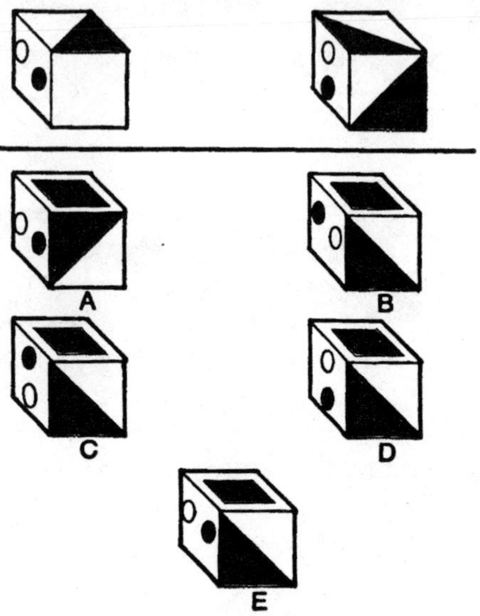

11 How many seven-letter words can you make out of MALICED?

12 Complete this series, giving a value for x.

11 13 17 25 32 37 47 58 x 79

13 Who is the odd woman out?

(A) MARGUERITE
(B) PRUDENCE
(C) FELICITY
(D) BEATRICE
(E) SALLY
(F) JENNY
(G) OLIVE

14 What letter should take the place of x?

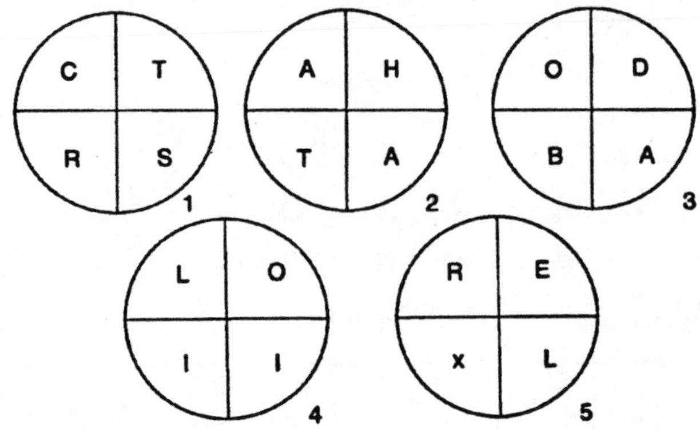

15 If A were placed on top B which of the outlines below would result?

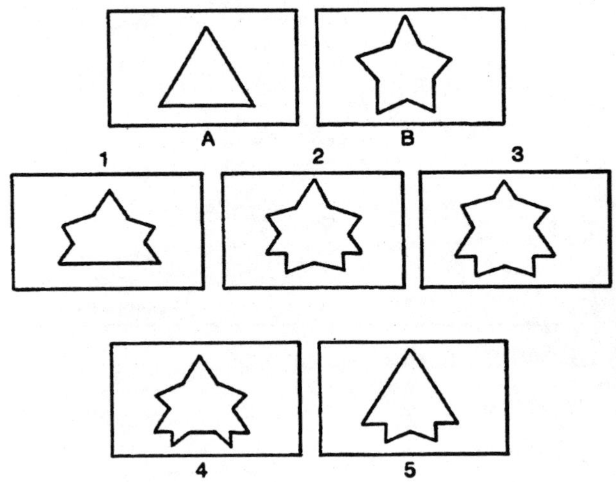

NOW CHECK YOUR ANSWERS AND KEEP A NOTE OF YOUR SCORE ON PAGE 62.

ANSWERS TO TEST 3

1 D **(SCORE 1 POINT).**
The figure is rotating clockwise.

2 (C) **(SCORE 1 POINT).**
The first and last letters of all the others are consecutive in the alphabet.
(A) BucoliC
(B) DiatribE
(C) Hourl
(D) JacK
(E) LocuM

3 The 9th spin **(SCORE 1 POINT).**
1st spin 19
2nd spin 3
3rd spin 9
4th spin 18
5th spin 32
6th spin 17
7th spin 27
8th spin 3
9th spin . . . . ZERO

4 K **(SCORE 1 POINT).**
Give each letter a value according to its position in the alphabet. The total value of the letters in CHOP (42) is the same as that in LARK (42). The total value of the letters in FREE is 34. The total value of the letters in DAR is 23, which means that the last letter must have the value of 11 to bring it up to 34. The 11th letter of the alphabet is K.

5 BIPEDS **(SCORE 1 POINT).**
Another problem based on the 26 letters of the alphabet corresponding with certain cards. Here clubs represent A to F (ace to 6); spades represent G to L (ace to 6); hearts represent M to R (ace to 6); diamonds represent S to Z (ace to 8). Therefore:

2 of clubs	B	(2nd letter)
3 of spades	I	(9th letter)
4 of hearts	P	(16th letter)
5 of clubs	E	(5th letter)
4 of clubs	D	(4th letter)
Ace of diamonds	S	(19th letter)

6 (D) **(SCORE 1 POINT).**
All the other words contain letters in alphabetical order.

7 AE; BG; CF; DH **(SCORE 1 POINT IF ALL ARE CORRECT).**

8 18 **(SCORE 1 POINT).**
Each modern number in any one segment has a number in Roman numerals in its opposite segment. Starting with MDC (1600), this is doubled in the opposite segment to give 3200. Moving clockwise, IV is halved, to give 2 in the opposite segment. This doubling and halving continues, so by the time we get to IX (9), this must be doubled in the opposite segment to give 18, expressed in modern digits.

9 D **(SCORE 1 POINT).**
These are the initial letters of the first five books of the Bible (the Pentateuch): Genesis, Exodus, Leviticus, Numbers, followed by Deuteronomy.

10 B **(SCORE 1 POINT).**
Examination of the top cubes reveals that they are rotating forwards (confirmed by the changed positions of the two spots on the side). As far as the facing side is concerned, B, C, D or E could be correct, but only in B have the two spots changed their positions in keeping with the forward rotation.

11 Four **(SCORE 1 POINT IF ALL ARE CORRECT).**
DECLAIM
CLAIMED
MEDICAL
DECIMAL

12 71 **(SCORE 1 POINT).**
Each number is increased by adding the total of its digits to the number itself. So, 11 (1+1=2) becomes 13, 13 (1+3=4) becomes 17, etc.
Following this procedure, 58 (5+8=13) becomes 71.

13 (D) **(SCORE 1 POINT).**

They are all women's names, but all except (D) are also nouns:

(A) MARGUERITE - the ox-eye daisy
(B) PRUDENCE - wisdom
(C) FELICITY - happiness
(E) SALLY - a going-forth
(F) JENNY - female donkey
(G) OLIVE - fruit

14 O **(SCORE 1 POINT).**

The circles contain four five-lettered words. Starting with C in the first circle, notice how the following letters move one place clockwise in each successive circle:

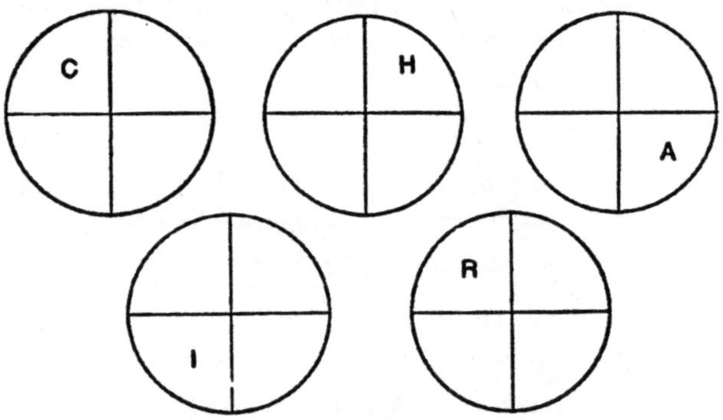

Starting with T in the first circle and proceeding in the same way, we get:

TABLE

Starting with S in the first circle, we get:

STOOL

Starting with R in the first circle, we get:

RADI-

Obviously, the only possible word that falls into the household context of the other words is RADIO, so the missing letter is O.

15 2 **(SCORE 1 POINT).**

Remember to keep a note of your score.

NOW TOTAL ALL YOUR SCORES FOR THE THREE TESTS IN THIS SECTION.

NOTES

A relatively easy test (to give your brain a rest after the hard mental work you have done so far!).

5 should have given little difficulty if you have followed the reasoning on previous problems of this nature. Many of our volunteers failed to get all four words in 11, the omission usually being DECLAIM. 3 and 14 gave the greatest difficulty, but all in all the scores were somewhat higher than in the previous tests in this section.

RATINGS AND IQ SCORES FOR GROUP III

TEST 1	Average 7 points
TEST 2	Average 7 points
TEST 3	Average 9 points

TOTAL FOR THE GROUP

(Out of a possible 45 points)

Over 39	Excellent
33-38	Very Good
24-32	Good
23	Average
18-22	Fair
Under 18	Poor

YOUR SCORES FOR MASTERFUL TESTS

TEST 1	______
TEST 2	______
TEST 3	______
TOTAL	______

SEE IQ SCORING INSTRUCTIONS ON PAGE 63

THE PUBLISHER'S SCORING INSTRUCTIONS

Count up the number of correct answers you received in the tests in each of the Elementary, Challenging and/or Masterful test levels. Find your approximate IQ score in the extreme right hand column. You may measure your IQ after one category of tests, or look to the sum of your scores for each of the test levels for your composite score after you have completed all three test levels.

NOTE: This chart is based on test-takers who are 16 years or older. If you are younger than 16, add 10 points to your score for every year your age falls below 16.

YOUR ELEMENTARY TEST SCORE	YOUR CHALLENGING TEST SCORE	YOUR MASTERFUL TEST SCORE	YOUR COMPOSITE TEST SCORE	YOUR APPROXIMATE IQ SCORE
60	60	45	165	140
59½	59	44½	163	138
59	57	44	160	136
58½	56	43½	158	134
57½	55	43	155	132
56½	54	42	152	130
56	53	41	150	128
55	52	40½	147	126
54½	51	40	145	124
54	49½	39	142	122
53	48	38	139	120
52	46	36½	134	118
50½	44	35	129	116
49	42	33½	124	114
47	40	31½	118	112
45½	38	30	113	110
44	36	28½	108	108
42½	34	27	103	106
41	32	25½	98	104
39½	30	24	93	102
37½	28½	23	89	100
36	27½	22	85	98
34½	26½	21	82	96
33	25½	20	78	94
31½	24½	19	75	92
30	23½	18	71	90
28½	22½	17	68	88
27	21½	16	64	86
25½	20½	15	61	84
24	19½	14	57½	82
22½	18½	13	54	80
21	17½	12	50	78
19½	16½	11	47	76
18	15½	10	43	74
16½	14½	9	40	72
15	13	8	36	70